Editorial

The Russian poet Ilya Kaminsky wrote about the previous war in Ukraine, in 2017:

Never (do you hear me – NEVER!) did anyone go after me for being a Russian poet and for teaching in Russian language in Ukraine. Everywhere I read my poems in RUSSIAN and never did I encounter any complications. However, tomorrow I will read my lectures in the state language – Ukrainian. This won't be merely a lecture – it will be a protest action in solidarity with the Ukrainian state. I call for my colleagues to join me in this action. A Russian-language poet refuses to lecture in Russian as an act of solidarity with occupied Ukraine.

Ukraine has made a few significant appearances in *PN Review*, usually as a place in which Poles, Russians, Hungarians and others unwillingly find themselves (in both senses). As an afterword to the translation he made, with Robert Pinsky, of Czesław Miłosz's 'The World: a naïve poem' (*PNR* 27, 1982) Robert Hass quoted from Miłosz's *The Captive Mind*:

In my wanderings at the beginning of the Second World War, I happened to find myself for a very short while in the Soviet Union. I was waiting for a train at a station in one of the large cities of the Ukraine. It was a gigantic station. Its walls were hung with portraits and banners of inexpressible ugliness; a dense crowd dressed in sheepskin coats, uniforms, fur caps and woollen kerchiefs filled every available space and tracked thick mud over the tiled floor. The marble stairs were covered with sleeping beggars, their bare legs sticking out of their tatters despite the fact that it was freezing. Above them loudspeakers shouted propaganda slogans. As I was passing through the station, I suddenly stopped and looked. A peasant family – husband and wife and two children – had settled down by the wall. They were sitting on baskets and bundles. The wife was feeding the younger child; the husband who had a dark, wrinkled face and a black drooping moustache was pouring tea out of a kettle into a cup for the older boy. They were whispering to each other in Polish. I gazed at them until I felt moved to the point of tears. What had stopped my steps so suddenly and touched me so profoundly was their *difference*. This was a human group, an island in a crowd that lacked something proper to humble, ordinary human life. The gesture of the hand pouring tea, the careful, delicate handing of the cup to the child, the worried words I guessed from the movement of their lips, their isolation, their privacy in the midst of the crowd – that is what moved me. For a moment, then, I understood something that quickly slipped from my grasp.

Ukraine first appeared in a translation of the Hungarian poet Miklós Radnóti, collaboratively rendered by George Gömöri and Clive Wilmer (*PNR* 4, 1978). 'The Fifth Eclogue' is a terrified elegy for a journalist who vanished during the Nazi occupation. The poem is a painful fragment.

My dear friend, how the cold of this poem made me shiver,
How afraid I was of words. Today too, I have fled it.
Have scribbled half-lines.
                              I tried to write about something – about
Anything else, but in vain! This furtive night of terror
Admonishes: 'Speak of him.'

'More than One View of Somewhere in Central Ukraine' by Horatio Morpurgo is a classic essay, a rolling stone that as time and history pass retains an alarming resonance, that news that stays news even as seasons, fashions and empires change. In this essay (*PNR* 20) he talks, among other things, about George Orwell, the brutal imposition of collectivised farming in the Ukraine and its thematic impact on *Animal Farm*. And he talks about the landlocked infancy of Joseph Conrad in Terekhove. Ukraine is a vivid and real place, overlaid time after time by brutalising politics, then emerging, then again submitting itself to the fate of all nations that lie at crossroads, places people move through that are seldom destinations in themselves. The Brazilian writer Clarice Lispector was born in Tetchelnick in the Ukraine in 1925 but stayed only a few weeks: her Russian-Jewish parents were emigrating to Brazil, and she occurred en route. A colourful placename, but not a place she ever returned to. About Terekhove and that other infant writer Joseph Conrad Horatio Morpurgo writes:

Back in the village where young Jozef learnt to walk, a cuckoo is calling and the caretaker scythes round a school building in the weekend quiet. A small space near its front entrance is marked off by a low fence, as if it was once a memorial garden. It is tulip time in Ukraine: this little rectangle is ablaze with scarlet, but whom or what did these blooms celebrate in tulip-times gone by?

News & Notes

History repeats itself • (from N&N, *PNR* 217, 2014) The *New Yorker* carried a report by Sally McGrane of the abuse of one of Ukraine's best-known poets and 'counterculture writers', Serhiy Zhadan. He was beaten up by pro-Russian demonstrators in Kharkiv, the second largest city in Ukraine, and images of his damaged face immediately circulated on the internet. 'As the attackers were hitting him, the writer said, they told him to kneel and kiss the Russian flag. "I told them to go fuck themselves," Zhadan wrote, on his Facebook page.' Sally McGrane notes how Zhadan's 'raucous poetry and poetic novels depict post-Soviet working-class lives in his country's rust belts; in his imagination, Ukraine's vast, rolling, sparsely peopled steppes and historically shifting western border are part of the country's vital essence rather than a point of weakness. He also fronts a popular ska band, "Dogs in Space"... Now, Zhadan is back in the hospital – his jaw has not been healing properly. But, he wrote in an e-mail, the beating has not deterred him. "It's very simple," he wrote. "I don't want to live in a country of corruption and injustice. I, like millions of other Ukrainians, would like to have a normal measure of power. A dictatorship is not normal, and people who don't protest injustice, they have no future."'

Valentina Polukhina • On 10 February we received news, from Emeritus Professor Joe Andrew of Keele University, of the death of Valentina Polukhina on 7 February at her home in London. She was a friend and major advocate of Josef Brodsky's, publishing as many as twenty books about his work, and was a significant translator (often with her late husband Daniel Weissbort) of leading Russian women writers into English. With Daniel Weissbort she produced the generous and comprehensive *Anthology of Contemporary Russian Women Poets* in 2005. She was also a vital presence in the London poetry and translation scenes. She went to the University of Keele in 1973 as a Russian Language Assistant and retired as a full professor in 2001. To *PNR* 203 (212) she contributed a translation of Mariya Galina's 'Ode to the Unveiling of Yury Gagarin's Statue in London'.

David Wagoner • *John Greening writes:* Just before Christmas, the death was announced of American poet, novelist, editor and teacher, David Wagoner (1926–2021).

An extraordinarily productive writer, who published his first collection in 1953 and his last fifty-nine years later, it seems apt that he is especially known for 'Staying Alive'. That poem's instruction-manual tone became a trademark, and *Traveling Light: Collected and New Poems* (1999) is full of such openings as: 'To walk downhill you must...'

Although he grew up during the Depression in industrial Ohio, Wagoner settled in Washington State, where he worked with Theodore Roethke, whom he considered a role model and whose notebooks he would edit. The influence is evident in poems about his father (and 'The Journey' could be from *The Far Field*), but Wagoner forged his own brand of eco-poetry. Invariably centred on Pacific Northwest landscapes and wildlife, it is timely and readable but seldom comfortable (vertigo, encounters with bears...).

Wagoner did not court disorder and he is missing from key anthologies whose editors favoured something less well balanced. Anger comes readily when writing about his father, but also on environmental matters – e.g. his furious addresses 'to Weyerhaeuser, the Tree-Growing Company'. But his strongest instinct was to laugh, as in 'For a Woman Who Phoned *Poetry Northwest* Thinking It Was *Poultry Northwest*' (Wagoner edited the former distinguished magazine for years). Indeed, he was a true entertainer, a gift perhaps inherited from his opera-singer mother, and had been a practising stage magician – experience which fed into his novel *The Escape Artist*, filmed by Coppola.

In later years Wagoner wrote elegiacally of love and fatherhood – two daughters arrived in his seventies, two collections in his eighties – softening the severity, reflecting rather than instructing. And all the while one of his very earliest poems was going viral ('Stand still' it begins) after Oprah Winfrey recited it online: without his knowledge, 'Lost' began to appear on T-shirts, in sermons and set to music. Thus the poet becomes his admirers.

Edmund Keeley • The leading translator of modern Greek poetry Edmund Keeley (who was also a novelist, teacher and poet) died on 23 February at the age of ninety-four. An obituary note will appear in *PNR* 265.

Reports

Sitting with Discomfort

Part II: Body and Word

VAHNI CAPILDEO

Is it possible to 'read' our bodies' reactions, when we are reading, and feed that into a literary appreciation of a poem's art? Do somatic responses simply indicate personal triggers, or are there patterns in our reading body that interplay with the text, not in a way that makes meaning from the text, but in a way that uncovers poetic form? I have been experimenting with a method of workshopping readings of the text via readings of the body. This piece will conclude by outlining the method. However, it is very new. To open up approaches beyond what I can perceive, I would like to retrace how I arrived at this type of reading.

First, a question: what image comes to your mind when you read the phrases 'sitting with discomfort', or 'sitting with difficulty', in connection with poetry? Are you literal-minded? Is it the image of a white cube art gallery with low-level, woven, circular seating? Is it the image of rustic benches with no backs in a dark upstairs room? Is it the pain of knees that will not lever an arthritic person up from the gallery's meditative, orientalist floor cushions? Is it the image of a crumbling spine rearranging itself inside an unsupported back, till nerves scream, internally drowning out any words?

Younger poets who live with chronic pain, invisible illnesses, or other disability, like Polly Atkin and Karl Knights in England, have not stayed silent about what it would mean for poetry, so often encountered via the 'poetry event', to be accessible. The 'Inklusion Guide', pioneered by Julie Farrell and Ever Dundas in Scotland during the unreckoned, spreading debilitation of the Covid-19 pandemic, is an evolving resource for best practice.

Did physical images come to your mind, with those words: 'difficulty', 'discomfort'? I remember my mother (now a wheelchair user) thirteen years ago, laughing at her own inelegance: she needed to carry a 'sports cushion' to arts events, and did not foresee that this was not a permanent solution; that one day, she would find herself excluded by her body from a shared life of the body and mind – wanting to have fun, but needing to rest in between dancing, and with no place to rest where fun was to be had.

I rather suspect that 'sitting with difficulty', 'sitting with discomfort', might bring to you the image of a poem that, in non-technical terms, you do not much like. There could be a lot of reasons for this; not least that, for today's poetry consumer, somewhere at the back of a successful poem lurks a nice and/or interesting poet, just about real enough to sign a book, and if the poem does not say who 'I' is, does not seem to have a face to meet your face, that is... difficult. Perhaps. There is also the matter of what the reader 'brings to the table'. This phrase conjures for me the image of a specific table, at an open-level poetry workshop. We were looking at a love poem and the pattern of pronouns. I felt moved to ask a non-abstract, academically illegitimate question. With love poetry that features an 'I' and a 'you', do you (as a reader who is also a writer) feel addressed as the beloved; do you feel able to speak as the lover; are you able to sound all the voices, feelingly but with detachment, like a playwright or director; or do you feel as if you are eavesdropping? A great clunky lesson dropped on my head: many readers felt as if they were eavesdropping, and these were also the ones who had sociological reasons not to 'fit' with that university, or with the implicit leisure of the intense lines. They cast themselves as overhearers of sonnets. Authors were somebody else. This, of course, was unspeakable.

More and more unspeakabilities lodged themselves in my mind via my body, in those years clustering around the year of 'Brexit'. At a book festival, a couple in an open-air café went out of their way to befriend me. They remarked, without asking, that 'my religion' was why I was eating 'that': pizza with mozzarella – instead of meat, like them. I did not write them up when reflecting on the festival. In the road outside my flat, a woman stood shouting. I thought she was unwell. It turned out that she was shouting at me for wanting 'us dead'. Brownly, I went indoors, drank a glass of water, and logged into a Skype meeting for the Out of Bounds project, on Black and Asian British poetry of place. I did not mention the anti-poem, the rant that tried to put me in my place. Gradually, I went from poetry engagement to scholarly meeting, feeling as if in a state of permanent jetlag.

I looked with other eyes at people in workshops and at readings. Each one of these listeners, readers, writers, was carrying so much else in and with them, additional to and perhaps resonant with the texts on which we ostensibly, also truly, focused. Perhaps these resonances were not distractions but clues to resonating points between the unspoken/unspeaking in individual human experiences and in the shareable poem? A host of expert witnessings pointing deep into the text, not traumatic reactions pointing back to self.

The workshop method I am developing consists in selecting texts with 'difficult' forms and/or 'uncomfortable' content. So far, we have looked at a Shivanee Ramlochan poem that exquisitely tears apart the power relations of rape; at a Dionne Brand poem that tenderly takes a long view despite and because of a young black man's murder; and Solmaz Sharif's stunning exposé of how militarised language that constructs her ancestral country as her adopted country's enemy corrupts the little lyricisms that would be natural to everyday family life.

I begin by saying that people can move around or stay still, leave, and come back, whatever makes them physically comfortable to hold their mental attitude of attention. Then, several times over, I slowly read out loud the text of one of these bloody, darkbright poems. We might share the reading out loud, but there is always at least one reading that I do while they concentrate. They have paper and electronic copies of the texts. I ask them not to try to understand what they hear, but to note their physical responses. They do not have to share any of this. I ask them not to try to focus on the text, but to note where they are distracted, and what the distractions are; note, without dwelling. Does the throat tighten; do they want to speak aloud; read some things over; skip ahead; when do they need to get up and walk about? Do they doodle, scrunch paper, look out the window, remember

something from childhood, or something they must do next? All this must be noted as co-occurring with the experience of the text.

What do we find? Complacent rejection of complicity in oppression, or guilty glorying in violence, shock or outrage crayoned monotone red and black? No; we find that the shifts in muscle tone and breath, the drift to the window view and back to the words, are in tune with deeper patterns than we had realised existed. People leave and come back without having to explain why; but it is in their notes, which remain theirs. It is surprising how often something in the poem's form coincides with a change in the reading body. For some, this inside-out collision of personal interiority and textual shape is a better diagnostic tool (as it were) of poetic form than having to articulate what they 'notice about the poem'.

This is how we all find our way to sharing that we are struck by Dionne Brand's inset and run-on sentence, in 'no language is neutral':

[...]   Each sentence realised or
dreamed jumps like a pulse with history and takes a
side.

Everyone notices a somatic response to these lines: a variety of responses, but at one distinctive stopping place. From our sharing, we work outwards to how the poem leads up to this moment: via the long and short sentences of a woman narrator who says again and again 'I have tried'. She has tried imagination, human and creaturely music, ceremony and veneration in the face of outrage. Now, here, she realises that the language we inherit is as intimate, infectious, sustaining and public as blood. Yet our pulses have jumped at this, not only from what she says, but according to the strong structures of her verbalisation. The poem itself concludes, pulsing with repetition that lengthens out into something more, that we may, indeed must, read through and with our bodies.

[...]
                not in
words and in words and in words learned by heart,
    told in secret and not in secret, and listen, does not
    burn out or waste and is plenty and pitiless and
    loves.

Our heart is more than that which can be shot or stabbed, or that keeps the machine going. Ungovernably, it is love and memory. Brand's 'faultless knowledge' of skin, drunkenness, and weeping is not a fancy way of praising emotion or elevating identity. It is an invitation to us to reconceive ourselves: creatures with speech and memory, with unspeakable, eloquent bodies. Civilisation may need revolution, but it does not need cities. This is authorship, the poem rebegot.

from *What Is Poetry?*

PHILIP TERRY

An artist takes two leaves and fixes them together with a paper clip. He calls the piece 'Bureaucracy'. The artist is the Catalan Joan Brossa. The piece is an example of one of his 'poem-objects'. This is not what we would normally think of as a poem. But if it is a poem it is perhaps because it presents us with likeness (as in the simile) and also unlikeness (also part of the simile, necessarily, though we sometimes forget this): the leaf is *like* the sheets of paper we file away in our filing cabinets (we speak of 'leaves' of paper), but it is also *unlike* paper. And it is in this unlikeness, as much as in likeness, that the force of the 'poem' resides, for while it seems natural to affix a paper clip to two sheets of paper, it borders on the absurd – and here we confront the surrealism of Brossa's work – to carry out the same operation on the leaves of a tree.

*

What is concrete poetry? Concrete poetry is not the same as concrete, but it has some similarities. Reading *An Introduction to Concrete Work*, with certain sentences I can substitute the words 'concrete poetry' for 'concrete', and it still makes good sense: 'If concrete poetry is to be strong, watertight, and durable it must be dense'; or 'If fresh concrete poetry is put in an oven it will dry out quickly and crumble to pieces.' With other sentences the sense is less clear: 'Simply stated, concrete poetry is a mixture of cement and other materials (known as 'aggregates') which sets in a hard mass when water is added'; or 'When concrete poetry is placed under water a tremie is used. This is a pipe with a funnel at the top and a valve at the bottom, and is sufficiently long for the funnel to be above the water when the bottom of the pipe is resting on the bed of the sea or river.' Even here, though, the result is a kind of poetry, even if it is not concrete poetry. Is poetry, then, what escapes when translating 'concrete' into 'concrete poetry'?

*

I remember at school we had a geography teacher called Mr Poole and that we sang 'Daddy Poole' to the tune of 'Daddy Cool' and that the whole class got lines: 'I must not sing Daddy Poole in class.' As we sat in the hall, hidden amongst the hundreds of lines we had to write out, we would insert phrases like 'I must not sing Daddy Poole can go fuck himself in class' etc. At the time this seemed like a harmless way of getting back at the teacher for overreacting to the situation, but now I'd see these *not to be read* lines as a kind of poetry – like poetry, they are quietly subversive, like poetry, they speak that which must not be spoken, like poetry, they reintroduce play into language, like poetry, they bear witness, like poetry, they are passed about among friends, like poetry, they turn defeat into celebration.

*

Buttonhole Poetry. To win prizes, your poetry should be of this type. It should not give off a bad smell. It should not be offensive. It should not be difficult. Historically, Ronsard is frequently of this type, whereas Villon is not. Most poetry, in fact, fails to meet these criteria somehow or other: Mallarmé does not give off a bad smell, nor is he ever offensive, but he is difficult. Ezra Pound, who never won any prizes, is difficult, offensive, *and* gives off a bad smell.

*

Poetry is not always where you expect it to be. It is almost entirely absent from the poems of Hermann Melville:

> No utter surprise can come to him
> Who reaches Shakespeare's core;
> That which we seek and shun is there –
> Man's final lore.

But it is everywhere in his prose.

*

Georgian Verse is to Romanticism what New Nature Writing is to Georgian Verse. The one closes the stable door after the horse has bolted, the other closes the stable door after the horse has bolted and the roof has collapsed. *Discuss.*

*

Making heavy weather of Emily Dickinson's poems, when I read this:

> Bee! I'm expecting you!
> Was saying Yesterday
> To somebody you know
> That you were due –
>
> The frogs got home last week –
> Are settled, and at work –
> Birds mostly back –
> The clover warm and thick –
>
> You'll get my letter by
> The Seventeenth; Reply
> Or better, be with me –
> Yours, Fly.

What else but a poem could do that?

*

'A poem is an expression of ideas or feelings in a language no one uses since no one speaks in verse.'
– Fernando Pessoa

*

Poetry takes us by surprise sometimes, as in the work of Anthony Etherin, where poetry takes on mathematical form in the shape of palindromes and anagrams. His 'Palindrome-Sonnet', one of two on the theme of *Frankenstein*, begins 'Deeds, lives allay me. Man...', and ends with the same letters in reverse order, so: '...name my all as evil's deed!' His 'Anagram-Sonnet', on the same theme, has perfectly anagrammed lines, the first two being: 'One scans Prometheus: I've taken fire; / A permanence of suns. I seek to thrive.' Both poems follow the lineation and rhyme scheme of the Shakespearean sonnet. Writing poems in this manner bears some resemblance to composing crosswords, but it is far more difficult, for the poet completes the crossword for us: the poem, consequently, must be more interesting for the reader than the reading of a completed crossword. It must be like a crossword which *also* works *as a poem*.

*

Different kinds of poetry: 'I remember Ezra reading one of his poems about a collection of jewels. "That's all right," my father said, "but what does it mean?" Ezra explained that the jewels were the backs of the books in his bookcase. Pop said, "If you mean that, why don't you say it?" I had a funny feeling about Pound; didn't know what kind of animal he was. I liked him but I didn't want to be like him.' – William Carlos Williams

*

'Every revolution in poetry is apt to be, and sometimes to announce itself to be a return to common speech.' (T.S. Eliot.) How true! Doesn't that account not only for the greatness of Dante and Chaucer, but of Wordsworth and Whitman, and of a host of more recent poets, from Olson to Larkin, Kerouac and Ginsberg? And yet, and yet. Revolutions in poetry are also apt to turn this idea on its head – Mallarmé's revolution was nothing if not a *retreat* from common speech.

*

Epitaphs. Recently I came across the following epitaph, in the churchyard at Alresford, Essex. It commemorates John Harwood, who died on 22 February 1827, aged 55:

Weep not for him who has no cause of tears
Hush then your sighs and calm your needless fears
If any thing in love to him is meant
Tread his last steps and your own sins repent.

In many ways this is utterly conventional of its kind, the stoically Christian sentiment, the rhyming couplets, the plodding rhythms. But seeing it *in situ* I was struck for the first time by the architecture which surrounds such epitaphs. The epitaph is inscribed on the upright gravestone, the top of which forms an arc, imitating and gesturing towards the sky above, while the body lies below, in the ground. In brief, the architecture gestures towards a threefold division of the cosmos: here on earth (where the epitaph can still be read on the gravestone), the heavens (above, in the sky), and the underworld, or, in the Christian world picture, Hell (in the ground). And this threefold division is echoed in the poem itself: the earth is where John Harwood trod 'his last steps'; the heavens, or Heaven, is where he is now, which is why he has 'no cause for tears'; Hell is gestured towards in the last line, it is the place you will go if you don't 'your own sins repent'. The epitaph, out of context, seems like little more than a conventional, even dull poem. But put it back in its context, and it is more like *an installation*.

*

It is often said that poetry is only flat when it is bad poetry – flatness, for example, is characteristic of a poor translation. On the contrary, poetry needs to maintain its right to be flat, flatness is part of its palette. Think, say, of a poem inhabiting a flat landscape – you do not want lines that bounce.

*

Common definitions of poetry: 'What oft was thought, but ne'er so well express'd' (Alexander Pope); 'Poetry is this space where every single particle of language is charged with the most meaning' (Ben Lerner). The first of these suggests that poets make their work out of the thought that already surrounds them, the art of poetry being akin to the art of polishing furniture. Here poetic language is *more polished* than ordinary language. The second statement, often wheeled out, suggests that poetic language is *fuller* than ordinary language, that it is distilled, dense, multi-layered, ambiguous. Both are true of some kinds of poem, but neither of these fit all poetry. Pope's definition leaves out the possibility that poetry might express what is otherwise inexpressible, just as Pope does in his best poetry, such as the *Essay on Man*. Lerner's definition leaves out the possibility that poetry might speak simply and directly, in the manner of common speech, as it does so often in the poetry of William Carlos Williams and Robert Creeley, even Wordsworth. And there is plenty of writing which fits these definitions which is *not* poetry: Quentin Crisp's memoirs are nothing if not highly polished; Lacan's psychoanalytic writings are highly charged in Ben Lerner's sense. The problem is perhaps that there is no such thing as 'poetry', that there are 'poetries', rather, and that even here poetry is constantly migrating, changing, exceeding and challenging our definitions of it. So that poetry, ultimately, cannot be defined. Poetry is in flight from 'poetry' as we understand it at any given time. Every book on poetry, in other words, like every definition of poetry, fails, and in this failure we find what matters most about poetry, its continuing life. So poetry can be 'rough' (Bill Bissett), 'uncharged' (Prévert). The poetry that is both rough and uncharged belongs to the future of poetry.

Bibliography

Brossa, Joan, *Poetry Brossa* (Barcelona: Macba, 2017).
Childe, H.L., *An Introduction to Concrete Work* (London: Concrete Publications Limited, 1952).
Dickinson, Emily, *Emily Dickinson's Poems: As She Preserved Them*, ed. Cristanne Miller (Cambridge: Harvard University Press, 2016).
Eliot, T.S., *On Poetry and Poets* (London: Faber and Faber, 1957).
Etherin, Anthony, *Stray Arts (and Other Inventions)* (Padstow: Penteract Press, 2019).
Melville, Herman, *Selected Poems*, ed. William Plomer (London: The Hogarth Press, 1943).
Pessoa, Fernando, *The Book of Disquiet*, transl. Margaret Jull Costa (London: Serpent's Tail, 1991).
Williams, William Carlos, *I Wanted to Write a Poem* (London: Jonathan Cape, 1967).

Oralism, Ableism and Counter Culture

LISA KELLY

If you allow poetry to do its real work to *learn and go on learning* – to steal from Cavafy's 'Ithaka' – your writing will take you on some unforeseen journeys. In 2016, I co-edited the Deaf Issue of *Magma Poetry* with Raymond Antrobus and chose the theme, having lost the hearing in my left ear through childhood mumps, but I knew little of Deaf culture or British Sign Language (BSL). Early on, my ignorance led to a sharp lesson. I cornered a well-known Deaf poet at an event and asked if he would like to contribute to the issue. When he realised I could not lipread nor communicate in BSL, I got his turned back for an answer. I resolved to take classes there and then.

Having grown up in the hearing world, where my deafness was something to be downplayed, negotiated, or joked about, I was never taught about Deaf culture or given the opportunity to learn BSL. In many ways things have not moved on. My brother-in-law trained as an audiologist and has no BSL skills. It is not offered as an essential part of professional development, and routinely deafness is treated as a medical problem which can be 'cured' with hearing aids or a cochlear implant. Such ableism denies opportunities that come with being part of a rich Deaf culture with its own language and history.

Some five years after my introductory course to BSL, where I painstakingly fingerspelled my name and learned how to sign 'thank you' – which millions can now do thanks to Rose Ayling-Ellis becoming the first Deaf celebrity to win *Strictly Come Dancing* – I progressed towards level 6 and a high-enough standard of fluency to be offered the role of CSW (communication support worker) for a Deaf supermarket assistant behind the lottery and cigarette kiosk at a major store on the Holloway Road. I had profound doubts about my abilities – not just my signing, but also my deafness. Being able to interpret from English to BSL relies on being able to hear what the customer is saying. I visited the store and ascertained that the queue of customers would be on my hearing ear, my right side, and that the acoustics were sympathetic, with low levels of background noise. Cupboards stacked full of cigarettes behind the counter created a protected space with no risk of someone behind me demanding attention to be heard. I accepted the job.

I wasn't sure what to expect from customers – how supportive or prejudiced they might be. During lockdown, I worked with two other Deaf poets, DL Williams, and Nadia Nadarajah, on a film-poem, *The House of the Interpreter*, for Nottingham Trent University and the Science Museum. We responded to an object from the Science Museum's collection from a D/deaf and marginalised perspective and chose an early telephone. During research into the telephony experiments of Alexander Graham Bell, his ableism loomed large. He is a notorious rather than a revered figure in the Deaf community. His wife, Mabel Gardiner Hubbard, was profoundly deaf due to contracting scarlet fever at age five, but he was convinced that Deaf people should be taught to speak. Years of being subjected to his Visible Speech therapy, a written system of symbols that instructed the Deaf to pronounce sounds, must have been a very refined type of torture. His ableist attitude reflected thinking about the importance of speech as 'a divine spark', and as essential for God to hear a sinner's confession. At the Second International Congress on Education of the Deaf – where only one delegate, James Denison, out of the 164 was Deaf – Bell voted with the majority to ban sign language in favour of the oral method for the teaching of the Deaf. This had a devastating impact on the Deaf community, and it has remained a sore wound.

Unfortunately, such prejudices about speech being what makes us human continue. My co-worker was signing to me and serving a man at the till. He asked me, 'Can she speak?' Before I could answer him and explain that we communicate in BSL, he added, 'It's wonderful she's been given a job. They are human you know.' I was left speechless and signless.

Yet, customers are often interested in sign language.

They frequently want to learn basic signs and say they wish they could take lessons. My current BSL teacher says enquiries about courses have shot up since Rose's *Strictly* win. Frustratingly, BSL is not offered as a GCSE course at schools and was only recognised as an official language by the UK government in 2003. It does not enjoy any legal protection, as do the Welsh, Gaelic and Cornish languages, although the BSL Bill is going through Parliament and if successful will change this. During the Covid-19 pandemic, we saw just how dismissive the English government is of its duty to provide a BSL interpreter for its scientific briefings on the coronavirus. A campaign was fought by Deaf activists, #WhereIsTheInterpreter, and a judge found that the UK government broke the Equality Act 2010. Culturally, however, BSL is beginning to receive more national attention and acclaim.

Poets including Ilya Kaminsky, Raymond Antrobus and DL Williams are raising awareness of Deaf poetics, culture and signing; and many events will ensure that BSL interpreters are provided for access, such as the recent T.S. Eliot Prize Readings at the Southbank Centre. However, interpreters' skills are not cheap and smaller poetry publishers and organisers often cannot afford BSL access unless the cost is part of a funding application. I have recently finished co-editing an anthology of poetry and short fiction by UK Deaf, deaf and Hard of Hearing writers, *What Meets the Eye,* with Deaf activist, playwright and actor, Sophie Stone for Arachne Press. The grant for interpreting the anthology from English to BSL could not cover the full cost, but through a fundraising campaign, the BSL translations are being added and will be the culmination of the first project of its kind in the UK.

The journey may have destination points along the way, but there is never a terminus. We have to keep moving forward, experiencing, learning, improving, and adding to our cultural and political awareness of what it means to promote and support sign language in what is ultimately an ableist culture. There is more work to do, more campaigning, no doubt with some setbacks, but within sight, there are huge gains. So much has been achieved. So much more will be achieved.

For those who are invested in the journey, there are riches to be found. Everybody's Ithaka is different, and perhaps the best we can hope for is a personal Ithaka that guides our development as poets and campaigners in unexpected and fulfilling adventures, whether initiated by redressing ignorance, injustice, or loss. Again, to steal from Cavafy:

Ithaka gave you the marvellous journey.
Without her you wouldn't have set out.

Andrew Waterman, 1940–2022

RORY WATERMAN

Below is the text of the eulogy delivered at my father's funeral at Colney Woods Burial Ground, Norwich, on 8 February 2022. He contributed to this magazine regularly for decades, from its inception until 2012. That was the year in which Carcanet ceased to publish his books, which he took as an affront. His final collection, By the River Wensum, *was published by Shoestring Press in 2014. He leaves behind a hurricane of difficulties that do not receive mention in the text below. Lazy comparisons between his poetry and mine often frustrate me, though I accept they are inevitable. And, much as I loved him, I hope nobody ever has cause to draw many non-poetic comparisons between us.*

*

This is the right place for my father's funeral, though sadly he has never been here before today. His best friend, at least as far as my father was concerned – who was one of the kindest men I've ever met and a true father and husband – passed away last summer, and had a very moving, well-attended funeral right here. Sadly, despite my best efforts, my father was unable to attend it, for reasons some of you know about. But that evening on the phone, as my partner and I stopped in Kings Lynn on our way back home to Nottingham, he asked me to describe the funeral to him. My father had an excellent imagination, so I'd like to think he saw it anyway, in his mind's eye.

My dad was born in London in 1940, just after the Phoney War had come to an end and just before the Blitz began. He was born to Irish parents, one of whom he later got to know and whom I called granddad. But he was adopted, and grew up mainly with his adoptive mother, my gran born in 1900, and then his younger sister – his wonderful younger sister. Until he was nine, he lived in Woodford, North London, with both adoptive parents, and then his mother moved with the two children to Croydon. He never saw his father again.

His favourite childhood pursuits were things like: climbing trees in Epping Forest, and later playing tennis in Ashburton Park; inventing tinpot dictatorships and then going to pretend war with his friend Chris (my dad's was Ludicrania, Chris's was Plonkvitia); running long distance races (pretty well, I gather); and, briefly, playing in a skiffle group, though he freely admitted to having no aptitude for music whatsoever, much as he liked listening to it. (When I was a child he'd give me tapes of folk music that he'd made, and later blues, both faces of each cassette bearing his characteristic almost-illegible scrawl of song titles on a thick layer of Tippex.) He was always the sort of person who'd like to have a go at things. But his childhood was complex, and so was he. At 17, and being a troubled and troublesome adolescent, he was ordered by police to leave the family home, and began several years of working at various jobs: bank clerk, bookshop worker, hotel porter. He took A Levels in his early twenties, then went to the University of Leicester to study English. He then began a DPhil on the poet Edward Thomas at Oxford, but left without finishing, because he'd secured a job as a lecturer in English at the New University of Ulster – first in Derry, and then in Coleraine. He arrived in 1968, just before the Troubles began in earnest.

In 1974, he published his first book of poems, *Living Room*, with Marvell Press. It was the first of ten books: eight collections, a *Selected Poems* and a *Collected Poems*. My dad was talented with words, the sleights they afforded, the control they gave him. Often, he rewrote truths, making them more manageable, then believing them. But he could also be poignant, moving, and funny: in one poem about gardening, he wrote: 'Concrete the bloody things over and leave yourselves free.' He might have said the same as a metaphor for the things he had done and seemed so capable of forgetting he'd done. But I think his reputation as a poet deserves to be higher than it now is.

He met my mother, his fourth wife, in 1980, when he was exactly the age I am now. Soon she was pregnant. His friends in Ireland hoped it would settle him, but it didn't: he wasn't one for being settled. She left him in 1983, and took me, a toddler, a wee wain, with her to Lincolnshire (thankfully). I think it is this distance that helped my childhood experiences of him to be so overwhelming, and they still are in my mind.

I'll always remember with passion our short, intense access visits when I was a small child, in Lincoln and elsewhere – including often here in Norwich. Him hiding behind the statue of King George III in Lincoln Castle and pretending to answer my questions in a gruff voice. Us making paper boats, decorating them with silly pictures, and racing them between bridges of the River Witham, unless the swans got them first. Him scurrying with me through the canopies of trees in the treehouses in the grounds of Belton House near Grantham. And, though I didn't then understand the implications, us sitting a while of an afternoon in the lounge of the Wig and Mitre pub in Lincoln, a pint on his side of the sticky little table, a glass of gloopy pineapple juice and ice cubes on mine, and a bag of cheese and onion crisps, dry roasted peanuts, or whatever, gaping in the middle.

And we'd go to football sometimes. He took me to my first game in 1988, at Carrow Road, with his friend Chris. Norwich lost 1–0 to Liverpool (those were the days!) and Chris got me Kenny Dalglish's autograph – but from that moment on, I was a Canary, and from that moment on, so was my dad. Have a little scrimmage, dad. Never mind

the danger. He always wanted us to cram as much as possible into those special monthly access visits and he was, in that respect, an inspiration.

He also told me, very frequently, that Ireland was my 'real home'. He'd put green t-shirts on me, emblazoned with the word 'IRELAND', and then take them back at the end of the weekend, because he said my mother would destroy them if he didn't. He also taught me words: judge, social worker, affidavit. I was semi-fluent in legalese at a surprisingly tender age. And I remember him proudly showing me a newspaper report, after he'd had a punch up at work with the Dean of Humanities. I didn't understand it, being about five at the time, but he assured me it was hilarious. This might not sound like excellent parenting. And it wasn't. But, along with the force of his personality, it all conspired to make him my hero when I was a little boy. He belonged to another planet, and I wanted to go there, and he wanted me to go there, and wanting didn't stop us from doing. Soon enough, I'd start to see him a little more as others did. And he didn't like that.

At the age of fifty, my dad was registered as a blind person, due to glaucoma. But he would downplay the blindness, telling people that – and I quote, I heard it often enough – 'in practice, I'm partially sighted.' How can anyone not admire that spirit? He didn't let partial blindness stop him doing *anything*. We'd hurtle up mountains in England and Ireland together, or navigate villages and towns and ruins and coasts in various parts of Britain and later continental Europe, his hand hooked in my arm so I might guide him. He'd take solitary holidays when I was in my twenties, and once strode purposefully off a jetty by mistake, landed up to his chest in water, clambered out, and walked back to his hotel, where he stood dripping in the lobby, proffered his hand for his key, and went back to his room. He'd fractured a bone in the process, but he thought the story at least equal parts funny and annoying, and told it to everyone for a year, punctuated by his characteristic abrupt laugh, the laugh he would use in any situation he thought warranted it, whether justified or not.

He retired in 1998, by then a senior lecturer, and moved to Norfolk – first to Cromer, where we'd spent lots of time when I was a child, and then to Norwich, essentially because his friends Chris and Joan lived here. He never returned to Ireland, and kept no friends there. Having not ever travelled abroad until the age of forty-two, with my mum and baby me to Austria, and rarely since, he felt he had some catching up to do, so he began going to different parts of Europe, and decided to learn Italian. He carried on writing poems. He listened to England cricket test matches whatever time of day or night, which I'll happily admit meant nothing to me, and to Norwich City games every week, after which he'd call and tell me excitedly what he knew I'd just seen or heard myself. It was a weekly ritual for decades, as the Canaries bounced around the leagues like a pinball. The last football match we went to together was about a decade ago, and he wore a radio headset tuned into Radio Norfolk, which I'd borrowed from my kind and beautiful mum. He could barely see the pitch, of course, even though we sat about three rows back so at least he'd get a shadowy glimpse whenever the ball came close. He was determined that it shouldn't matter, as always. (And we beat Forest 2–1 that day, which both of us regarded as particularly pleasing, because I'd recently become a resident of Nottingham and had taken a slightly dimmer shining to 'the other NCFC', Notts County.)

In 2018, having made some more characteristically unwise decisions, he turned in on himself for the last time. His friends worried, as he repeatedly took to bed with bottles of wine, fell asleep at dinner tables, and at one point slipped over on the way back from Tesco, bottle in hand, and ended up in hospital. And in April 2020, early in the first lockdown, overwhelmed with disappointments, he again found himself on his own. By this time, he was clearly unwell, and almost totally isolated. Eight months later, he was taken to hospital, diagnosed with metastatic colon cancer, and given twelve weeks to live. But my father was built of tough stuff. He lived for thirteen months more, and for twelve of those at Twin Oaks Nursing Home. The staff there – Sonia, Sue, Bena, Eppie, and all the others – were superb, the sort of people who restore your faith in humanity in an instant. He wasn't in a condition to show gratitude, but I like to think an earlier version of him might have done, at least if the care had been provided to someone other than himself. The same is true of his friend Paolo, who always tried to give my dad sage advice and sincere help, despite the odds. Thank you for being a true friend to my dad, Paolo. And the same to you, Joan. He adored you. And he was right about that.

My dad lost his final optimism in October, when he discovered he'd been blocked from any prospect of going home. Going home was all he really wanted to talk about last year, and the dementia caused by his alcoholism made him even more assiduous on that point. He knew I tried everything I could to get him live-in care at home, despite my reservations about how safe he would then be, and I hope that offered some comfort, however cold. Nobody could get through to him by telephone in his final weeks: he'd usually just croak 'later' when the receiver was brought to him, and yelp if it wasn't taken away again. The last time I saw him, a few days before he died, a phrase from one of his favourite Philip Larkin poems came to mind: 'that whole hideous inverted childhood'. His penultimate words to me that day were 'lots of love. Best wishes.' He died alone, having spurned food for weeks. Cancer would have killed him, but hopelessness got there first. His heart broke.

I loved him passionately, though it was not always easy. His alcoholism waxed and waned, and at times he fought it gamely. At others, less so. He made a great many mistakes, enough for several lifetimes. Even so, few thought he would make the mistake he ultimately did, which I won't name, and he deserves deep sympathy as well as other emotions: his life could have been so much more than it was. But for the moment I'd prefer us to remember him as the optimist he had often been throughout the preceding seventy-five years. In his later life, until recently when it was made impossible, we'd still talk all the time about a million things, then email one another at considerable length too. He kept up several detailed correspondences with others, as well. If he was interested in something personally, he'd talk and talk and talk. If he wasn't, he'd let you know, and tut impatiently. But *we* liked so many of the same things that we always got by, and ours was the only very close family relationship of his life that endured through decades. My dad was also very supportive of my own early attempts at writing, about twelve or fifteen years ago: he'd want to see my drafts, and if I let him he would make suggestions, whether I asked for them or not. Some were terrible. But all were made with pride. He'd send me his own drafts, and no doubt some of my suggestions were terrible too – he sometimes thought so. But we were two writers. He liked that. And so did I. And I admired his talent.

But, as a folk song we both loved, puts it:

It's not just what you're born with, it's what you choose to bear.
And it's not how large your share is, it's how much you can share.
It's not the fights you dreamed of, it's those you really fought.
And it's not just what you're given,
it's what you do with what you've got.

Good night, Dad.

Mrs Bleaney

JOHN CLEGG

Here's the opening of 'Mr Bleaney'. Larkin's prospective landlady is speaking:

> 'This was Mr Bleaney's room. He stayed
> The whole time he was at the Bodies, till
> They moved him.'

This does seem to present a mystery – or at least an obliqueness, a turning away from something. I'll go on to offer a theory about what the landlady is turning away from, but first, I want to give an account of exactly what she means here, or rather the limits to what she might mean.

Larkin gives his own account of 'the Bodies' in a letter to Alan Bold: 'I was brought up in Coventry, a great car-making town, and there used to be works there which we referred to rather by what they produced than the names of the makers. "The Bodies" was a fictitious example of this, invented for its macabre overtones.' (It is not all that fictitious; Carbodies, which made the chassis for London taxis, was operating out of Coventry during Larkin's childhood.) For the two main Coventry car companies, Jaguar and Standard, all the manufacturing happened on the same site, although Jaguar initially bought their engines from Standard. The only possible ambiguity in the landlady's speech comes in the final clause: 'till / They moved him'. Some critics have read Larkin's 'macabre overtones' as a full-fledged double meaning – he's been moved on from the Bodies, i.e. he's died – and so have been keen to read 'they' as doctors, undertakers or similar. I don't think this can hold: from the landlady's words, surely all the syntax allows is for 'they' to refer back to 'the Bodies'. 'They moved him'. Who? His bosses at the factory. Where? To some other part of the company. (He can't, for instance, have been made redundant; then she'd have said 'moved him on'.)

But this opens up a question of its own: why, having been moved to a different role in the same company, did Mr Bleaney change his accommodation? It can't have been for an easier commute: as we've seen, while some car bodies were manufactured by specialist companies, the large factories didn't outsource their bodies. If Mr Bleaney had been working for a large firm like Jaguar or Standard, a move would have been to a different part of the assembly line on the same site. It can't have been to save money: the poem makes it very clear that the 'hired box' Larkin is considering is at the absolute bottom of the rental market.

There is one obvious answer, I suggest, as to why an employee at a car factory in the 1950s would move out of their rented accommodation immediately after changing jobs: because they'd got married. 'They moved him' – he was promoted, and with the addition to his salary he decided he could marry the person he was in love with.

We get one more sentence of the landlady verbatim ('Mr Bleaney took / My bit of garden properly in hand'), then have to reconstruct her indirect speech , but it isn't difficult: the speaker of the poem has been informed relentlessly about Mr Bleaney's 'habits – what time he came down, / His preference for sauce to gravy', etc. Leaving aside what these details tell us about Bleaney ('every word a bullseye', was Larkin's later verdict), what can we reconstruct of the character of the landlady? I suggest that she is slightly resentful; she wants to show off how well she knew Mr Bleaney, how attentive she was to him, while insinuating that perhaps the new Mrs Bleaney doesn't share this attentiveness. Read in this way, she becomes something real, and the otherwise vapid fifth stanza redeems itself. It also accounts for her obliqueness at the start. 'They moved him' (to a new position), because she doesn't want to go into the way in which he moved himself (out of her lodging house).

This interpretation would, I think, have been news to Larkin, both as the speaker of the poem and its author. He *was* aware that he might have made Mr Bleaney too cheerful for the identification between himself and the poet which the poem gestures towards: 'the last third is reassuring myself that I'm not [becoming Mr Bleaney], because he was clearly quite content with his sauce instead of gravy, and digging the garden and so on', Larkin said in a 1981 interview, 'and yet there's doubt lingering too, perhaps he hated it as much as I did'. The hypothetical Mrs Bleaney exists among those points of doubt; the poem was a favourite among Larkin's readers, somewhat to his surprise, and it seems fitting to me that its protagonist had a larger existence than Larkin was aware of. (One further example of this larger existence: Mr Bleaney encouraged his landlady to buy a radio: 'the jabbering set he egged her on to buy'. Archie Burnett, in the endnotes to his magnificent edition of the poems, lists a hundred examples of Larkin complaining about the sound of radios through thin walls in hired rooms – an unpleasant room, for Larkin, contained a semi-audible radio on principle. But there's also a reason why Mr Bleaney chivvied his landlady to buy one, a reason I think Larkin wasn't aware of: so he could listen to the 'four aways' that he bet on in the football pools.)

One of the great successes of the poem is Mr Bleaney's name: it shares with J. Alfred Prufrock the capacity for summoning up an entire character. (Larkin had taken it from a lecturer at Oxford.) It surely works through associations of sound: bleak, bleary(-eyed), lean, the diminutive suffix -*ie* (as in *teenie-weenie*). But one other association might have been on Larkin's mind when he began the poem. A few months earlier, he'd finally completed 'Toads', a poem he'd been working on for almost a decade. The poems share a similar argumentative movement in their finales: the idea that 'something sufficiently toad-like / Squats in me, too', and that 'something' being what keeps the speaker tied down to an utterly mundane life and death, is surely a making explicit of the shivery half-identification at the end of 'Mr Bleaney'. It is something which

> [...] will never allow me to blarney
> My way of getting
> The fame and the girl and the money

All at one sitting,

as Larkin writes in the penultimate stanza of 'Toads'. 'Blarney' and 'Bleaney' surely at least suggest one another, and 'blarneying' (Merriam-Webster: 'persuade using charm or pleasant flattery') is surely one thing which Mr Bleaney is good at ('the jabbering set he egged her on to buy'). In my reading, the girl and the money are what Mr Bleaney has blarneyed himself into. The 'fame' he'll get later, from Larkin.

Letter from Wales

SAM ADAMS

> But here, on a rock blanched by it,
> The sun prints the shadow of a fern,
> Still as a fossil, pointed like an arrowhead:
> The mottoed tablet to an aeon.

This swift sketch conveys an intuition of deep history in its image of rock and shadow. Although the stone appears 'blanched' by sun, the poet is not treading chalk downlands, with clear trout streams and forested distant views. He is in a yet more ancient landscape and responds to it with strangely reminiscent vigorous turns of phrase, as if he had already imbibed a strong dose of Anglo-Welshness:

> The beck strikes down,
> Jabbing wittily through narrows.
> [...]
> Bleached pates of rock, shreds of foam
> Dull beside quartz, the sunstone glittering.
> At intervals, unscoured rock piles
> Keep a laboured quiet like sacked monasteries.

The lines are from 'Landscape', one of two sequences (the other, 'Elegy for the Labouring Poor') preserved in Jeremy Hooker's *The Cut of the Light – Poems 1965–2005* from his first solo collection, *The Elements*, published by Christopher Davies in Swansea in 1972. The latter, a 'Triskel Poets' pamphlet, was among the earliest I edited following Meic Stephens' gift of the series to me. *Snow on the Mountain,* Gillian Clarke's first, was in the same batch.

Appointed to the English department at UCW Aberystwyth, Hooker came to Wales in 1965. To a young man, chock-full of words, buzzing with creative energy, I fear his posting was less than congenial. In a recent interview in the on-line magazine *Wales Arts Review*, he says he found the department 'rife with tensions'. Having observed one or two of the personalities involved at fairly close quarters, albeit from a student's perspective, I believe I have some inkling of the situation he encountered. Perhaps that was what prompted him to move out of the town, for in a while he settled in a village about nine miles south of Aberystwyth. Llangwyryfon, with a population probably less than five hundred at that time, was rural certainly, but in the foothills of upland mid-Wales, and in almost every respect quite unlike his home in southern England. The language of the hearth and neighbourly communication was (and, despite the iniquitous spread of second-home ownership, to an extent possibly still is) Welsh, and it was close enough to the coast to be exposed to the ferocious westerlies that autumn and winter bring whipping in from Cardigan Bay.

Having come to Wales not knowing there was a living Welsh language, or an Anglo-Welsh literature (Edward Thomas, so far as he was concerned, being a poet of rural England), he set about gaining some familiarity with the former and with the work of Welsh writers in English, who, much as now, received scant recognition from the metropolitan hub of literary England. He also began sounding out Welsh journals. The first magazine he approached was the *Anglo-Welsh Review*, and he found in Roland Mathias a discriminating and warmly appreciative editor. No sooner had he caught the editorial eye with two poems and an article on Edward Thomas (in Vol 18, No. 41) than he found himself in the next number given the freedom of Roland's concertina-like spread of pages to write a long review article on a new major anthology of Anglo-Welsh poetry, *The Lilting House*, edited by Meic Stephens and J.S. Williams (1969). It was rare at the time to have the views of an 'outsider', still less one possessed of both empathy and sound judgement, brought to bear upon a substantial sample of fifty years of Anglo-Welsh poetry. The review set a high standard for literary discourse and, even when critical of standards, it at least offered reassurance that the work had been taken and considered seriously.

Having written dozens of letters and posted parcels of books to the address in my capacity as reviews editor for

Poetry Wales, I clearly recall Jeremy's home in Ceredigion was 'Brynbeidog'. No street name or house number was needed: there was only one 'Brynbeidog' in Llangwyryfon. To him it was a place of 'elemental beauty' – 'a small stone house in a third of an acre of ground, surrounded on one side by sycamores and open on the other to the hills, in a wedge between two mountain streams, named from its proximity to one of them, the Beidog'. The description is taken from 'Living in Wales', an autobiographical essay published in the magazine *Planet* in 1974. When things got on top of him, as they did from time to time, he found relief in cultivating his garden.

Ned Thomas, who had returned from lectureships in Salamanca and Moscow to become a thoroughly amiable and engaging colleague in the English department at Aber, launched *Planet* in the summer of 1970. Along with the *Anglo-Welsh Review* and *Poetry Wales* (not to mention the fifty-seven contributions to *PN Review*), it immediately became another outlet for Hooker's prolific production of poems, reviews and articles. The Aber years were formative in terms of what became for him key texts, the work of writers whose sensibility involved above all a melding of response to landscape with religious belief, including Edward Thomas, John Cowper Powys, Alun Lewis, David Jones, Roland Mathias and R.S. Thomas. His commentary upon and analysis of their work made a vital contribution to the early years of scholarly study of Welsh writing in English in Welsh universities. At the same time he was establishing himself as a poet with *Soliloquies of a Chalk Giant* (1974) and *Landscape of the Daylight Moon* (1978) from Enitharmon, and *Solent Shore* (1978) and *Englishman's Road* (1980) from Carcanet.

Jeremy Hooker left Aberystwyth to take up posts in Winchester, the Netherlands, Bath University, and the United States, before returning to Wales and the University of Glamorgan/South Wales, from which he retired as emeritus professor in 2008. He now lives at Treharris, about eight miles from the university campus, mostly up the road towards Merthyr Tydfil and that memorable sequence of apostrophised spots on the map, Fiddler's Elbow, Traveller's Rest and Quaker's Yard. In recent years he has suffered ill-health, including two lengthy spells in hospital between June 2019 and August 2020, during which he has written journals and poetry. *The Release* (2022), published by Shearsman, is the latest. The title alludes to a 'creative release', the 'lyrical stream... released in [his] mind' during the time in hospital. In large part, this turns upon 'soul, spirit, breath of God' and brings him back, again and again, to the art and thought of David Jones, 'a crucial figure' in these times, when 'we lack connection... to one another, to nature, and to God'. Elsewhere he writes, 'What I long for is language of the real, as in Clare, actual fields & working landscape, real dirt, not "flowery" words.' Perhaps it is through this envisioning of the real that, although in thought he still revisits his childhood home, as we all do, he can write of 'the warm, practical humanity... in the communities in which suffering and fellowship have 'forged' (that industrial metaphor) a people', and feel 'at home' in South Wales.

A Parochial Pessoa

COLIN BRAMWELL

Fernando Pessoa described himself as 'a drama divided into people, instead of acts.' Richard Zenith's recent biography thus begins with Pessoa's major *dramatis personae*: no less than forty-eight fictional authors. The majority of these characters were bit parts, but others were more prolific, establishing themselves in their creator's psyche. These lingering presences became Pessoa's 'heteronyms' – a coinage that implies a far greater degree of separation between real-life author and *nom de plume* than is usually supposed. This game of inventing fictional authors appears to have been established in the poet's childhood. Pessoa was born in Lisbon, but spent his formative years at a British public school in Durban, where he began sending his poetry to local newspapers under the name of Charles Robert Anon (a later English heteronym was named Alexander Search.) After his schooling was over, he returned to his city of birth, and never left. He didn't have to. At least two of his heteronyms were quite well-travelled.

Pessoa's five major heteronyms are Bernardo Soares (author of *The Book of Disquiet*), and the four poets represented here: Alberto Caeiro, Ricardo Reis, Álvaro de Campos, and 'Fernando Pessoa'. All write in Portuguese, all exist in the same extended universe, and all, with the exception of Caeiro, are prolific, though it is Caeiro who provides a philosophical underpinning for the rest. His doctrine holds that there is no such thing as hidden meaning in the observable world: each thing is only what it is, and nothing else beyond. In *Disquiet,* we come across an account of Caeiro's effect on Bernardo Soares:

'I experience a feeling of inspiration and liberation as I passively reread those simple lines by Caeiro that tell what naturally results from the smallness of his village. Since it is small, he says, there one can see more of the world than in the city, and so his village is larger than the city...'

This insight of Caeiro's should be central to our understanding of Pessoa's relationship to the English-speaking world, where he is now well known in translation. Although Pessoa never fully turned his back on the language of his education, his most enduring work was written in Portuguese, by the Portuguese heteronyms. Patrick Kavanagh famously drew a distinction between 'provincial' and 'parochial' artists: while the 'provincial' defers to general opinions from the metropolis on all matters, artists with a 'parochial mentality' are 'never in any doubt about the social and artistic validity of [their] parish.' I would argue that Caeiro – and, by extension, Pessoa himself – evinces a parochial understanding of his own practice. This may be inspiring and liberating for any poet, as it was for Soares, but will be particularly felt by those of us who, like Caeiro, come from small places, and/or write in languages other than English. We all know that writing poetry can be an obscure business, and choosing to write poetry in minority or endangered languages can, at moments, exacerbate this sense of obscurity. But Pessoa does give a sense of what remaining in one's own parish may be worth to us, ontologically as well as linguistically. Whoever we are, wherever we are from, whatever language we speak, will be sufficient.

Sadly, when translating Pessoa's work into 'standard' English, it is difficult to give a sense of his pre-existing engagement with the Anglosphere, or of this corresponding parochial mentality. The qualities that make Pessoa genuinely special – his playfulness and sense of humour, his authentic melancholy, his uniquely staid brand of irreverence – don't always survive the journey into the deterritorialised form of language that still predominates in the sphere of literary translation into English. My own choice of target language for Pessoa is not entirely intended as a counterblast to this sort of thing. Scots is far too often reduced to being a thorn in the elephant's paw, rather than seen as its own, albeit more diminutive, elephant. But something about the peculiarly double context of Scots works for Pessoa.

Scots poetry is most often read (in Scotland and elsewhere) within an English-language domain. It is also normally disseminated and evaluated in said domain, and thus may appear somehow foreign *and* intelligible to English-speaking readers. Simultaneously, Scots exists in its own sphere, with its own registers, idioms and vocabularies, and this sphere has in turn existed at various degrees of separation from/overlap with English throughout history. To borrow Lawrence Venuti's useful terminology, this means that all Scots translations will, to a greater or lesser extent, foreignise English within an English sphere, *and* domesticate the translated language within its own. Which is to say, Scots will always be a good choice of language for any poet with a vexed relationship to the English-speaking world. (Which may be all of them: including, I suspect, the English ones.) Certainly, there is a natural level of verisimilitude between Pessoa's relationship to English and that of Scottish poets like Robert Garioch, for example, who was educated in and mastered English, but who wrote all of his most significant work in Scots, and is therefore not well known outside of Scotland. Like Pessoa, many Scottish writers have a foot in two separate linguistic camps, and so there is sometimes a feeling of existing *ni de aqui, ni de alla* – neither from here, nor from there. This, as Pessoa's work demonstrates, can also be a type of parochial feeling.

I started translating Pessoa into Scots because I had a sense that certain time-honoured registers of the language might fit well for some of the heteronyms; and that translating others might usefully stretch my own sense of what the language might be good for. *Saudade*, the Portuguese sense of bittersweet longing, translates quite easily into a Scots context where sentimentalism and a conspicuous move towards song are established threads of discourse. These threads are present in all of Pessoa's heteronyms, but most pronounced in the work of Álvaro de Campos. Campos's pervasive longing is thus relatively easy to accommodate, as is the scenery he likes to chew: the Scots vocabulary is well-equipped for both urban and maritime settings. Ricardo Reis is a similar case. In order to translate his formalised disaffection into Scots, I thought of his relationship with classical poets, and mapped this onto MacDiarmid's relationship with Dunbar, Douglas and the 'golden age' makars. MacDiarmid distilled the influence of these poets into profound lyrics of comparative brevity; in Scots, Reis proceeds along similar lines, formally and tonally. For Caeiro and Pessoa, I couldn't think of any readily-match-ing voices or registers. I tried to translate Caeiro into a more neutral but still recognisably west of Scotland way of speaking, and to speak as plainly in Scots as I could. Regarding Pessoa, I bring him closer to my own way of speaking in the language, allowing a northern accenting of certain words to creep into as standard a West-Mid Scots as I could find.

I was determined not to fall victim to the excessive veneration that writers of renown can elicit from their English translators. Some risks were taken: locations, objects, foods transposed. '*Dobrado á modo do Porto*' became 'Cullen Skink'. To my mind, encountering either dish cold would be similarly unpleasant, and the latter was funnier, more meaningful in the new context. Ultimately, the goal was not to turn Pessoa into a Scottish person, but rather to make him sound like a person, or people, from *somewhere*. The reader can judge my success in this regard. I understand that the experience of reading Scots can be uncanny for English-speaking readers. For those who worry about finding Scots hard-going on the page (it's always far easier if you read it out loud) I refer you to the following, from a speech by Franz Kafka, made to the German-speaking audience at a Yiddish poetry reading. 'There are active in yourselves forces and associations with forces that enable you to understand Yiddish intuitively. Once Yiddish has taken hold of you and moved you, you will have forgotten your former reserve.'

Bibliography

Kafka, Franz, 'An Introductory Talk on the Yiddish Language', *Reading Kafka: Prague, Politics and the Fin-de-siecle*, ed. Mark Anderson (New York: Schocken Books, 1989).

Kavanagh, Patrick, 'Parochialism and Provincialism', *A Poet's Country: Selected Prose* (Dublin: The Lilliput Press, 2011).

Pessoa, Fernando, *Obra Édita*, http://arquivopessoa.net/. Accessed 01/05/2020.

Pessoa, Fernando, *Selected Prose*, transl. Richard Zenith (New York: Grove, 2001).

Pessoa, Fernando, *The Book of Disquiet*, transl. Richard Zenith (London: Penguin Classics, 2015).

Zenith, Richard, *Fernando Pessoa: An Experimental Life* (London: Allen Lane, 2021).

ALBERTO CAEIRO

Frae 'The Keeper o Sheep'

XX

The Clyde is bonnier

The Clyde is bonnier than the river rins throu ma toun –
But the Clyde isna bonnier than the river rins throu
   ma toun,
Acause the Clyde isna the river rins throu ma toun.

The Clyde hus mony faur-kent ships
But, fur thaim wha see in ilka thing whit isna there,
The memories o thae ships
Wull sail it yet.

The Clyde rins doun frae the megins o Lanarkshire –
New Lanark, Larkhall, Blantyre, Rutherglen,
   Clydebank,
An eftir Gourock tuims intil the sea.
We aw ken this.
But fewer o us ken whit the river o ma toun is cried
An whaur it comes frae

An whaur it gangs.
Bein the belangin o far less
The river o ma toun is muckler an mair free.

The Clyde wull wise ye tae the warld.
Ayont the Clyde thair's America
An the fortunes o thaim wha foond it.
No man in ma toun hus iver thocht
Ayont the river.

The river in ma toun disnae gar ye think o muckle:
Thaim that staund forby it, staund forby it.

XXXIX

The mystery o things

The mystery o things: whaur is it, syne?
Hou come it winna jist shaw itself,
So we micht ken it's a mystery eftir aw?
Whit dis the river ken o it, whit kens the tree?
An whit dae I ken – I, wha isna mair than they?
Ilka time I luik at things an think aboot whit men
   maun think
I mak a soond like a river strickin stanes afresh.

Acause the anely hiddelt meanin o things
Is that things dinnae huv a hiddelt meanin.

An here's the cuiriousest o ilka cuiriosity –
Mair antrin than aw the dwams o aw the poets in the
   warld melled thegither
Or even the thochts o the metaphysicians –
Ilka thing is anely whit it is.

Aye, here's whit I've divined frae ma ain gumption –
Things dinnae huv meanin: they huv existence.
The anely hiddelt meanin o things is things.

The bairn that thinks aboot an lippens tae fairies

The bairn that thinks aboot an lippens tae fairies
Is actin like an infirm god, but aye a god.
Fur in spite o his uphaudin the claim that no aw things
   exist,
He kens hou things exist: by existin.

He kens existence exists ootside o explanation
He kens thair's no reason fur onythin tae exist
An he kens that tae exist is tae exist at wan position.
He jist doesna ken that thinkin's no a position.

Lest nicht, the preacher o truths

Lest nicht, the preacher o truths
Spake wi me agin.
He spake o the poverty an sufferin o the warkin clesses
(No that o the impoverished, whar mair likely tae be poor).
He spake o the injustice o thaim wi cash tae spare
While ithers hunger. I didna ken whit type o hunger he meant:
It's possible tae hunger fur anither man's puddin.
Oan an oan he jawed aboot the things that fashed him.

Hou happy maun ye be tae think sae aften o the sadnesses o ithers!
An hou stupit no tae ken that the sadness o ithers belangs tae them
An winna be cured frae ootwith:
Real sufferin's no the lack o ink
Or a kist withoot an iron trim.

Yammerin oan aboot injustice is like girnin aboot deith.
I winna fash my airse tae fecht
Anent whit's cried injustice in the warld.
Gin ye'd mairch a thoosan staps,
Ye'd jist huv maircht a thoosan staps.
I thole injustice as I thole a stane fur no bein roond
Or a Scots pine fur no bein anither type o tree.

I speld an orange intae twa unequal pairts.
Tae which wiss I unjust – I, wha planned tae eat them baith?

RICARDO REIS

Folla oot yir destiny

Folla oot yir destiny,
Watter yir plants,
Luve yir roses.
The rest are scaddows
O the trees o ither fowk.

Reality's
Aye whit we're eftir,
Gie or tak.
Except that we're aye
Equals o oorselves.

It's guid tae live alane.
An gallant, an grand
Tae live semply.
Leave yir pyne oan the altar,
Saicrifice it tae the gods.

Haud life in the hyne-aff.
Dinnae be quaistenin it.
Thair's no a thing
It can tell ye. Yir answer
Is ayont the heivens.

Bit doucely imitate
Olympus, in yir hert.
Gods are anely gods
Acause they dinnae
Think aboot whit they are.

Hou muckle douth an daurksomeness

Hou muckle douth an daurksomeness
Drouns oor peerie-heidit lives!
   Hou aften has oor nippit luck
   Owerwhalmed us stick-an-stowe!

Happy is the beast wha doesna ken itself,
Wha slochs in green fields an walcomes
   Deith like a hamecomin;
   Or learned fowk, tynin

Themselves in science, heezin thair daeless, ascetic
Lives abune the lives o ithers, like a reek that hauds
Its moullert airms up tae the croun
O a lift that doesna exist.

Here, wi nae ither Apollo than Apollo

Here, wi nae ither Apollo than Apollo,
Lat us abandon Christ withoot remorse:
   As whun yir gods are shilpit an twafauld
   Ye airt thaim oot, an the trail gangs cauld.

Far flung frae Christian sensuousness,
The chaste lown o an eldern beauty
   Retours us noo tae aulder furms o strife:
The muckler mense that we cry life.

ÁLVARO DE CAMPOS

Cullen Skink

Wan day, in a café ootwith space an time,
I ordered luve, an received a bowl o cauld broth.
Tentily, I telt the missionary o the kitchen
I'd liefer it hot,
As broth (an it wiss Cullen Skink) isna eaten cauld.

Syne they startit gittin aw fuffy, like.
Appearantly ye canna be richt ony mair, no even whun
   yir the customer.
I didna eat it, didna order onyhin else, jist peyed fur it
An left, syne raikit up an doun the street ootside.

Wha kens the meanin o this?
No me, an its ma story an aw.

(Bit I dae ken well eneuch that in the universal
bairnheid
there is aye a gairden,
Private or public, or aiblins belangin tae a neebour.
An likeweys I ken this gairden, back in the day,
wiss mair the property o oor fun,
As sadness maun belang tae the category o 'present'
   alane.)

I ken aw this an aw,
But gin I asked fir luve, hou cud they ser me
A bowl o cauld Cullen Skink?
It's no a thing ye can eat cauld,
But they brung it cauld.
I didna girn aboot it, but it wiss cauld.
Ye canna eat it cauld, but they gave it me cauld.

I leant back in the deck chair an appened ma een

I leant back in the deck chair an appened ma een,
An destiny keethed in my saul like a crag.
My past an futur lives guddled thegither.
Midship, I heard a soond frae the smokin lounge:
The game o chess is dune, I thocht.

Swey,
Kittle o the tide.
Sweelt
In the hap o a day that isna morra yet –
The hap o bein ootwith duty fur noo,
O no huvvin a personality, but findin somethin o
maself here
Oan this chair, like a buik – like that buik yon Swedish
   quine forgat...

Sunk
Inwith idleset fantices, a bittie nodsome,
Lithesome, unrestfu...
An the likeness o myself appears as a bairn langsyne,
Pleyin oan the ferm, an kennin neither the algebra o
   mathematics
Nor the Xs an Ys o sentiment.

Ilka pairt o me is langin
Fur that insignificant maument
O ma life.
Ilka pairt o me is langin fur that maument an its
    likenesses:
Mauments whaur I didna reck,
Mauments whaur I kent the hail vacuum o existence
    withoot the mynd

tae try an unnerstaund it,
An thair wiss mune an sea an lanesomeness. *Aw,
    Álvaro.*

I alichtit frae the train

I alichtit frae the train,
An said *ta-ta* tae the new pal I'd made.
We'd been thegither fur eighteen minutes.
The crack wiss guid.
Fraternal.
I wiss sad tae leave him ahint.
Casual, man. I never thocht tae ask his name.
It felt like ma een were wavin him aff wi ma greetin.
Ilka fareweel is a deith.
Aye, ilka fareweel's deith.
The hale o us oan the train we cry life
Bein casual tae wan anither,
An sorrafu whun time comes tae alicht.

As I'm human, ilka human thing muives me.

Ilka thing muives me acause
I amna componed o ideas or licht,
But hiv a true an muckle commonweal wi aw
    humanity.

The aumous Seamstress wiss ill-used by the hoose
But aye left greetin.
She didna want tae leave...

The hail o this inwith my hert, aw the deith an
    waesomeness o the warld.
The hail o this lives an dees inwith my hert.

An my hert's a bittie muckler than the hail universe.

FERNANDO PESSOA

Frae 'Lashin Rain'

VI – 'The conductor waves his baton'

The conductor waves his baton,
Beginnin the sluggish, dulesome tune –

I mind a day, back in my bairnheid it wiss,
Whaur I wiss playin in the gairden o ma auld hoose

Thrawin this ball aroon. Mind it hud oan wan side
A fleetin green dug, an oan the ither
A blue horse wi a yelllow rider –

An on the tune conteenas. But noo it seems
Ma hail bairnheid is keethin tweesh me
An the conductor as a white gairden wall.
The ball retours, syne the green dug's seen,
Syne the blue horse wi the yellow rider –

The concert hall is the gairden o my auld hoose, my
    bairnheid is
Aw ower the shop, the ball retours an it's pleyin a tune,
A dulesome tune that enters the gairden
Dressed as a green dug keethin intae a yellow jockey –
(The ball aye spins tweesh orchestra, an I –)

I cast the ball oot at my bairnheid,
It stravaigs the hail o the concert hall at ma feet
Pleyin wi a yellow rider an a green dug
An a blue horse that keethes at the ither side
O the gairden wall – an this tune's thrawin the ball
    back
Tae my bairnheid – an the gairden wall is made
O batons an jabbelt green birlin dugs
An blue horses wi yellow riders –
The hail concert hall is a white wall o music
Whaur a green dug gies chase tae nostalgia
Fur bairnheid an a blue horse wi a yellow rider –

An frae wan side tae the ither, frae richt tae left,
Frae whaur the trees begin, frae their heichmaist
    branches
Whaur the baund pleys frae their nest,
An frae the toyshelves in the shop whaur I erst picked
    oot that baw
wi the green dug,
The shopkeeper smiles, happit inwith memories o
    bairnheid –

An the music staps like a wave crashin doun,
An the ball rolls doun the craig o an interruptit dwam,
An frae the back o a blue horse, the conductor, a
   yellow jockey turnin black,
Thanks me, hings his baton oan a wall that's winnin
free,
An bends doun wi a smile, wi a white ball balanced
   oan his heid,
A white ball vanishin ahint his back –

I dinna ken hou mony sauls I've gat

I dinna ken hou mony sauls I've gat;
I cheenge at ilka maument.
I'm aye antrin tae maself.
I've niver seen or foond maself.
Gin ye've a saul, ye canna be still.
Gin ye see, ye anely see yirself.
Gin ye feel, ye dinna.

Alert tae whit I am an whit I see,
I cheenge intae *thaim*, an no maself.
Ilka dwam o mine, ilka wish
Belangs tae wan wha isna me.
I'm ma ain laundscape,
I watch maself passin by:

Orra, ambulatory, alane,
Unable tae feel maself.

An that is hou I've come, bi accident,
Tae read my ain life as a buik.
No kennin whit'll happen,
An forgettin whit hus happened else.
I tak tent o a note in the margins
O this buik: a feelin, scrievit doun.
Noo I read it ower, askin 'Wiss that me?'
God kens, mun: he scrievit it an aw.

Autopsychographical

Aw poets are actors,
An ilk acts so sevendibly.
They'll even act oot akes
O akes they're feelin in reality.

Readers o a poet's script
Encoonter pain that isna real;
They swap the twafauld pynes o life
Oot fur a pyne they dinna feel.

Roond an roond its whippit track
The dance staps an restarts:
Twa train charrits made o string:
A model fur oor herts.

Glossary of Scots Words
(in order of appearance in the poem)

megins – depths
tuim – empty
gar – compel
forby – besides
maun – must
antrin – strange
fash – bother
thole – suffer
aye – always, forever
douce – sweet
douth – gloom
peerie – small
nippit – tight
stick-an-stowe – completely

sloch – slobber
tyne – lose
daeless – pointless
moullert – decayed
shilpit – pale
airt oot – seek
mense – intelligence
souch – peace
lown – calm
eldern – ancient
fuffy – testy
tentily – carefully
raikit – paced
keethe – appear

guddle – mix/confuse
kittle – tickle
sweelt – swaddled
hap – cover/blanket
lithesome – mild
win free – escape
orra – peculiar
sevendibly – thoroughly

Tarn and Wall and other poems

ANGELA LEIGHTON

Tarn and Wall

I'd set out in sun to reach that shore –
  the climb's surprise
among the higher fells, its wide-open eye
  a bowl of ice-melt
brimful, sky-struck, a cup for the gods –
  but found instead
this Damascene stop – a blindness sudden
  as the unread rock

of a sheltering wall topped with slate –
  each upright blade
a transverse fipple to the wind's ways
  each hearting-stone
a keeping lock to baffle the rain's
  crosswise slam
and a driven pashm of mist everywhere
  infilling the visible –

where all I find is a coating of star-moss
  galaxies of green
the tiny life's clinging resilience
  and a dry-stone wall's
soaked reserves of stony minerals –
  my one gain to be
crouched to the coldest thing – like a tomb –
  learning to see.

Ditty for the Poets

For *hornlight* (Hopkins) – moon's gold-sound in sight.
For *slughorn* (Browning) – long slog to an old note.
For *soodle* (Clare) – a sidling and slow mooch.
For *quicket* (de la Mare) – fast peepshow of laughing.
For *quoof* (Muldoon) – warm dream-hood in darkening.

Let them catch at a blue moon once in a while,
and reach so high across soundwaves crossing
that nothing's to know and knowing's a full
earful of wonder – where sense cuts a caper
with noise, and a nonce-word resounds ever after.

Calendula Sicula

Chaff, I think, and shuffle a pack of dormant stuff
won from forgotten depositions, from centuries of death
in chalk and limestone – barely, see? an advance on dust –
discovered in a drawer like a lost love-letter, this comfortless Easter.
I read its faded envelope again: Pantalica, 07
and think how gardens flower about the dead in their rented sepulchres.

Sicilian marigolds, earthy aureoles, reaped from the cliffside's
plundered tombs, a future countdown in survival's calendar –
this cold Good Friday of a year of deaths, I recall them flourishing
in buttonholes of bone, bonny in the sunlight's open prospect.
From buried dust, a corolla of gold – Mary in marigold.
From earth's stone, the flit of a ghost – anthem in chrysanthemum.

Cyclamen at the Winter Solstice

Something... I forget –
     something the brain hunts backstairs for
in cobwebby haunts
     a neural cubby-hole that has shut its door.

I'm offguard, distracted
     by this arabesque of fans, a pinwheel turn-around
(which flipside's right?)
     flunkey to the cold moon, pearl on the ground

yet winging it, very still –
     flung from a whirlwind into this world,
thin wrapper, litter,
     love-letter sugar-spun, whiteness unfurled?

Yet something... I forget –
     standing waylaid by this light-flare dancer
icy marker
     of a dark path growing longer and harder,

by a grace so utterly
     careless, other, so obliviously keen
that I stand accused
     of being here, still needing to explain.

Dear winter survivor –
     (how many now dying?) I might live to know
forgetting's a life gift.
     I came for something... Is it time to go?

Skyspaces

ROWLAND BAGNALL

Gigantic Cinema: A Weather Anthology (Cape) £14.99

'– the day goes on, a strange, wild, smiling, promising, lowering, spitting day – full of threats and contradictions'
– Walt Whitman

'This is an attempt to pull a book through without weather,' suggests Mark Twain at the beginning of his novel *The American Claimant* (1892), in which all atmospheric 'intrusions' are banished to an appendix – 'out of the way' – from which the reader is at liberty to 'help himself from time to time'. Twain's gripe, however tongue-in-cheek, is that the appetite for weather as a 'literary specialty' is getting out of hand. 'Many a reader who wanted to read a tale through was not able to do it because of delays on account of the weather,' he writes, while 'Nothing breaks up an author's progress like having to stop every few pages' to check in on the forecast.

'Of course weather is necessary to a narrative of human experience,' he concedes, but it ought to be put 'where it will not interrupt the flow,' a comment about the relationship between plot, digression, and stagnation that shares something with another famous observation credited to Twain: 'Everybody's talking about the weather but nobody's doing anything about it.'

While it might be too simplistic to frame *Gigantic Cinema* – a recent anthology of weather-related (and -adjacent) writing co-edited by Alice Oswald and Paul Keegan – as evidence of somebody finally doing *something* about it, the collection certainly embraces weather's plotless and digressive nature. Presented as a twenty-four hour cycle of unending, shifting, changing states – an 'omni-form day, containing all weathers', suggests the preface, borrowing a phrase from Coleridge – the three-hundred entries included here not only span the different stages of a single day (from dawn to dusk and back again) but also slide their way over a full range of meteorological effects, emphasising the sheer, alive ongoingness of weather, a wave of 'non-stop interruption'.

This process is represented by an equally impressive breadth of texts, from the literary to the scientific; poetry, yes, but also extracts clipped from novels, essays, letters, journals. Scholars of Alice Oswald's work will be excited by the possibility of finding some original translations here, with all unattributed examples noted as the labour of the editors, but the success of this collection lies in its surprises and collisions. There are plenty of old favourites – Hughes's wind, Apollinaire's rain, even Chaucer's 'shoures soote' – though these turn out to be familiar faces in a crowd of unexpected guests, from Joan Didion and Frank O'Hara through to Edvard Munch and Wittgenstein. Stripped of their titles, the authors' names pushed to the bottom of each page, the entries start to melt into each other, 'one excerpt summoning up the weather of the next', according to the editors. As such, the snow from a slice of Bachelard's *Poetics of Space* (1958) falls into a poem by Norman MacCaig, snow-flaking its way through passages of Yoshida Kenkō's fourteenth-century *Essays in Idleness* and the diary of Reverend Woodforde before settling over Captain Scott's Antarctic journal and a scene from Chapman's *Iliad*. Pliny's eruption of Vesuvius is followed shortly by a fragment of Don DeLillo's *White Noise* (1985). Later, the 'delicate and threadbare' rains of Francis Ponge appear to fall from Roy Batty's interstellar monologue during the closing scenes of *Blade Runner* (1982): 'I've seen things you people wouldn't believe.'

Despite its twenty-four-hour billing, the anthology comes to emphasise the peculiar timelessness of its subject. Phasing from extract to extract, one is aware of jumping backwards and forwards over centuries, as if the collection somehow offered a glimpse of all times happening at once, the past, present, and future playing out their weathers simultaneously. One thinks of John Ashbery's poem 'Into the Dusk-Charged Air' (not present here), in which each line utters the name of a particular river: the poem is intensely linear, flowing from source to sea, each river inherently related to the forward movement of each line; at the same time, however, 'Into the Dusk-Charged Air' is entirely simultaneous, a snapshot of the globe at one specific moment, as though every line were spoken in the same breath as the rest.

Alongside its expanding and contracting temporalities, *Gigantic Cinema* also raises questions about what – if anything – all this weather has to do with us. One cluster of entries draw explicit (often religious) connections between the weather and human activity, as in the rain-making rituals of various indigenous communities (recorded in *The Golden Bough* [1890-1915]), or the gods of Greek mythology producing weather in response to men. In an entry consisting of a Royal Proclamation, Charles II decrees a 'publick Fast' in order to reverse a recent bout of national flooding, a last-ditch attempt 'to divert those Judgements which the sins of this Land have worthily deserved'. In the following passage, John Evelyn connects the appearance of a whale swimming up the swollen Thames with the death ('That year') of Oliver Cromwell. Even Banquo's assassination in *Macbeth* (1606) appears to trigger atmospheric consequences – 'It will be rayne to-night' – just as Duncan's earlier murder conjures up a supernatural darkness: 'by the clock, 'tis day, / And yet dark night strangles the travelling lamp'.

Stranger than these, perhaps, are passages in which the distinctive flavour of the weather – so often unseen and unregistered – is rendered suddenly significant. The anthology is filled with moments of startling and striking human experience, scenes of fragility and violence, to which the weather seems inherently attached. A storm of 1773 that may otherwise have been forgotten sticks in the mind of Gilbert White because it kills a lady's coach-horse. Elsewhere, Defoe pauses over the wind-stripped lead of Lytton Church, blown from the roof, 'rolled up like Sheets of Parchment'. 'Once I faced the reflection of my own face in the jet-black mirror' of the train window, writes Rudyard Kipling: 'When the fog thinned, I looked out and saw a man standing opposite the pub where the barmaid lived. Of a sudden his breast turned dull red like a robin's, and he crumpled, having cut his throat.' Most staggering of all is an anecdote from the operating table, in which a surgeon brings procedures to a sudden, unexpected halt, gathering his team to view 'an extraordinary local rainbow effect' occurring in the patient's body.

'After all, what is not weather?' ask the editors, who include a wealth of other entries detailing intriguing possibilities, from starling murmurations to the bombing of Hiroshima. '[M]eteorologists are discussing the possibility of a connection,' wrote Alexander MacAdie in the pages of *The Atlantic Monthly*, between 'the tremendous expenditure of ammunition' in Europe during the First World War and 'the records of excessive raininess during the winter of 1914–15'. 'In concise terms,' he wonders, 'has the bombarding not only caused clouds but forced the clouds to send down rain?'

While many authors listed here seek to discover a relationship between the human and the atmospheric, the reverse side of the coin is to imagine pure indifference, like the great, cavernous clouds dominating Turner's painting *Snow Storm* (1812), in which Hannibal and his men are being hopelessly engulfed. Prominent extracts in *Gigantic Cinema* express the bold theatricality of weather – an 'Atmospherical Theatre', in the words of Thomas Appletree – for which we are the audience. 'I have often thought of writing a set of *Play-bills* for the vale of Keswick,' writes Coleridge in his notebook, 'announcing each Day the Performances by his Supreme Majesty's Servants, Clouds, Waters, Sun, Moon, Stars, &c.' This idea is nowhere more pronounced than in Virginia Woolf's 'On Being Ill', an essay of 1926 from which the anthology borrows its title. 'This then has been going on all the time without our knowing it!' writes Woolf, considering the 'shocking' sky:

– this incessant making up of shapes and casting them down, this buffeting of clouds together, and drawing vast trains of ships and wagons from North to South, this incessant ringing up and down of curtains of light and shade, this interminable experiment with gold shafts and blue shadows, with veiling the sun and unveiling it, with making rock ramparts and wafting them away – this endless activity, with the waste of Heaven knows how many million horse power of energy, has been left to work its will year in year out. [...] One should not let this gigantic cinema play perpetually to an empty house.

Like the sky that she describes, Woolf's writing vibrates with 'endless activity', a pageant of images traversing her stage, coming and going with 'incessant' unfinishedness, an 'interminable experiment' of 'veiling' and 'unveiling'. Framed, in part, by illness's invitation to pay attention to the world anew, 'to look round, to look up', she writes, 'perhaps for the first time for years,' framed even by the rectangle of window that one sees through from one's sickbed, Woolf discovers in the sky something inherently cinematic, though also something which – however we may like to think so – 'has nothing to do with human pleasure or human profit'. 'If we were all laid prone, frozen, stiff,' she continues, 'still the sky would be experimenting with its blues and golds.' Not just a cinema, but a cinema in which the film is playing whether we are there or not.

The disinterested sky of Woolf's essay brings to mind *The Clock* (2010), Christian Marclay's ambitious twenty-four-hour film installation, a real-time collage of clippings from movies in which the time of day appears on screen, an artwork that serves, in its way, as a useful analogue to Oswald and Keegan's project. I am reminded, also, of the Pantheon in Rome, whose oculus – a circular opening at the centre of the building's dome, seen in Panini's painting (c.1743) – offers a permanent view of the sky's 'endless activity'. More than these, however, *Gigantic Cinema* evokes the work of veteran American artist James Turrell, whose Skyspaces encourage viewers to perform the kind of looking Woolf's essay promotes. These site-specific chambers, typically smooth concrete interiors – there are more than eighty internationally, including three in the UK – present a framed, uncovered aperture, completely open to the air, through which the colours, shifts, and contours of the sky reveal their overlooked complexities.

While learning how to be attentive to the weather – to really *look*, as Woolf would have it – might be achieved through practice, the problem of how to translate one's attention into writing is a challenge of a different kind. One solution might be discovered in the language of precision, as in the attempted scientific classifications of Francis Beaufort's 'Wind Force Scale' or Robert Hooke's descriptions of the 'faces of the Sky', both present here. 'It is [...] desirable,' urges Hooke, 'that the particulars may be entered [...] in as few words as are sufficient to signifie them intelligibly and plainly.' And yet, 'It must be remembered,' as Dr Johnson reminds us, that 'words are hourly shifting their relations, and can no more be ascertained in a dictionary, than a grove, in

the agitation of a storm, can be accurately delineated from its picture in the water.' How can we ever hope to write about something a slippery as the weather, this anthology appears to ask, with something as slippery as language?

There comes a moment in any review of an anthology, I suspect, when the reviewer complains about the absence of some key passage or other, a missing author who ought to be present, a poem whose absence undermines the project. Oswald and Keegan make it clear that their selections are a drop in an ocean, emphasising their preference for 'writing which is "like" weather', 'As if the weather were to write itself', reminiscent of Yves Klein's eccentric attempts to capture 'the mark of an atmospheric occurrence' by exposing empty canvases to rain. Some of the anthology's most successful moments are those that seem to share this spirit, presenting writing as immediate, unfixed and changing as its subject which is particularly true of the many rapid-fire notebook jottings on display from Hopkins, Whitman, Coleridge and Clare, to name a handful. As Gilbert White puts it in a letter of 1776, perhaps 'The most certain way to be exact' about the details of a 'remarkable frost' is 'to copy the passages from my journal, which were taken from time to time as things occurred'. This immediacy – moment to moment, 'time to time' – acts as the guiding principle of the selections here. I am reminded of the word 'trans-shifting' – 'To shift and then be shifted by that shift' – which Oswald singles-out from Herrick in her inaugural Professor of Poetry lecture at the University of Oxford, available online. In the words of the Polish poet Wisława Szymborska: 'I'd have to be really quick / to describe clouds – / a split second's enough / for them to start becoming something else.'

Despite my best efforts to resist the anthology-reviewer's cliché, the emphasis on natural writing as a (trans-)shifting, fluid, even living thing leaves me surprised not to find Emerson here. Criticism of Emerson's prose very often comments on its distinct, unstable quality. Indeed, 'Like the weather,' writes Eduardo Cadava, it 'moves and happens according to the rhythms and crises of its own atmospheres, storms, and pressure zones. Like the weather, whose variable and unpredictable nature makes it difficult to circumscribe, the gestures of his writing [...] resist, from the very beginning, all our efforts to bring together or stabilize whatever we might call his "thought".' 'He looms up like a thunder cloud,' suggests an anonymous reviewer of 1849, then 'comes down in a shower of tinkling sleet and rolls away like a fire on the prairie.'

Nevertheless, *Gigantic Cinema* stands as a great and full achievement, establishing an essential bedrock of weather-related writing with which to help make sense of our own ongoing changing climates. More than this, it strikes at the heart of poetry's greatest and oldest subject, mutability. After all, 'We are the changing inhabitants of a changing world,' writes Emerson: 'The night & the day, the ebbing and flowing of the tide, the round of the seasons, the waxing & waning moon, the flux & reflux of the arts & of the civilization of nations & the swift and sad succession of human generations, these are the monitors among which we live.'

Tunes for Bears to Dance to

STUART HENSON

'Language is a cracked kettle on which we beat out tunes for bears to dance to,
while all the time we long to move the stars to pity.' – Flaubert

$\left\{ \begin{matrix} 2 \\ 4 \end{matrix} \right.$

Wrong stop. Wrong foot. Wrong turn. Wrong place.
Wrong suit. Wrong time to play the ace.

Wrong man. Wrong church. Wrong vow. Wrong girl.
Wrong speech. Wrong joke. Wrong choice of words.

Wrong house. Wrong street. Wrong door. Wrong day.
Wrong lie. Wrong truth. Wrong every way.

$\left\{ \begin{matrix} 3 \\ 4 \end{matrix} \right.$

The slap of the stick and the kick of the drum.
The drag of the chain and the strain of the song.
The blood on the sawdust. The weight of the light.
The rime on the straw in the frost-eaten night.

The laughter of children. The pity of whores.
The maggots that creep in the pads of his sores.
The silence of stars as they weep through the black.
The dogs in the box-car. The rats on the track.

The feet without claws and the jaws with no teeth.
The pap in the bucket. The shit-stink of meat.
The pits of his eyes and the depths of his rage.
The rust-roaring stains on the bars of the cage.

$\left\{ \begin{matrix} 4 \\ 4 \end{matrix} \right.$

Word   weird   wired   welt
Stave   starved   spat   spelt
Tread   tied   toyed   trolled
Step   strap   script   scald

Trip   tap   trope   twist
Jest   just   jerk   gist
Sign   signifier   stress
Paws   parse   pause   press

$\left\{ \begin{matrix} 6 \\ 8 \end{matrix} \right.$

Under the light of a moon like an old kettle
pitted and potted and made of a soft metal
Bear goes out dancing and beating his tambourine
(mud makes and marks every pace like soft plasticine)

Next day police with their notebooks and spy-glasses
follow his passage through damp woods and salt-
    marshes –
out to the beach where the trail of his minuet
washes away like a song that the world forgets

Carl Phillips in conversation

IAN POPLE

IP: Why and how did you start writing? And how long did it take you to trust both your imagination and your own voice? Also, a supplemental question: I know your mother was English; did she retain her accent, and if so, might those cadences have affected your voice, spoken or written?

CP: I always wrote, as a child growing up, for pleasure. I kept diaries, I created a family newspaper where I wrote all the articles and did the cartoons, and then distributed copies to my parents and sisters; and I wrote poetry throughout high school and college. I should mention that my mother wrote poems, usually occasional poems – she'd write a poem for my birthday, or a Christmas poem, that sort of thing. So I grew up with poetry seeming a perfectly normal thing to be interested in... After college, I didn't write for maybe seven years, had no desire to do so. I had also gotten married to a woman, and had no clear idea that I was in fact a gay man – I wouldn't have married, had I known that. But at some point in the marriage I began to understand the reality, and it was a point of crisis – I didn't want to hurt my wife, I couldn't make sense of my feelings, I didn't want to be unfaithful. I suddenly began writing again. I believe now that the poetry saved me, maybe literally.

As for trusting imagination and my own voice... I guess it hasn't ever occurred to me not to trust my imagination. And I don't know, to this day, if I really know what is meant by voice – I have always just written the way I think, which seems natural to me. It wasn't until I started publishing books that I got a sense that how I saw the world and how I wrote about it were somehow different from how others do it. But that, too, seems reasonable, we each have our own sensibility.

Which leads me to your supplemental question. My mother did retain her accent – I never noticed it that much, of course, since I grew up with her, but as soon as we'd leave the house, she would always be asked where she was from, asked to repeat things so people could hear her accent, etc. But because she didn't seem to me to sound like anything but who she was, I think it seemed as ordinary as my father's speech, with his accent from Alabama. I don't see any traces of these things in my writing. My speaking voice is a different matter. I have often been asked where I'm from – as in, what country – and I have also often been told that I sound a bit snooty, which is how Americans often hear British accents. So I suppose maybe my speech has been affected? But that could also be the effect of having gone to a snooty university! Who can say?

Do you feel a connection between the spoken voice and the written one – in general, and in particular with your own voice?

I can probably only speak accurately about my own voice. For me, the voice in my poems is the same as the voice I speak with, has the same cadences, has the same tendencies towards longer, looping sentences punctuated with revision, self-correction, pauses for thought... And I guess I've always assumed this is how it is for every other poet. Certainly when I've met a poet, I've usually not been surprised by how they speak, if I'm familiar with their poems.

Do you read your poems aloud as you write them?

No, but I read them aloud constantly while I'm revising. I tend to write in a big block of what looks like long-lined prose. When revising, I say everything out loud as a way to determine where the lines might break, what sounds like a natural pause. This involves many handwritten drafts. When I'm close to what feels like a final draft, I type it out on the computer – at that point, my line breaks often shift, depending on how I feel about the overall look on the page, but also I sometimes find, once I type it out, that what I thought needed long lines – or short – now seems to work better with a different line length. Meanwhile, I don't mark stanzas until I've got a draft on the computer. But I don't need to work out loud for stanza breaks – just for line breaks. The other reason for reading the poem aloud is that I often don't realize until then that I have too long a stretch of the same kind of rhythm (seven dactyls in a row, for example), things I missed until I heard the work out loud, places where the metre (even though I only write free verse) needs to be roughed up a bit more, or sometimes smoothed over...

What poets have influenced you, and were those the same poets you were reading in your early writing days? What, in particular, were you getting from those writers, do you think?

I have a very wide range of influences, more than I could list here. I've usually pointed to four large categories of influence. The first is classical literature, specifically Greek tragedy. It's from those writers that I came to understand tragedy as existing at the point where how we wish to behave comes into direct conflict with how we are told or expected to behave by society. This turns out to be exactly where my poems live, which makes sense, since they speak – especially the early work – to queerness and to Blackness, both being things that tend to resist societal expectation. Race has especially been part of this, though it doesn't appear in the poems much – but I have spent my life being told that I'm not quite Black, not quite White, that I sound White, that I'm in denial about my Blackness, that I look unspecifically 'foreign'. So, I think Greek tragedy helped me find where my poems live, and gave me much of my subject matter.

Next is my stumbling upon a book of William Carlos Williams's selected poems back in 1985 or so, which was my introduction to 'contemporary' poetry. I had no idea that poems could be written that sparely about such seemingly ordinary things.

Around the same time, I became acquainted – in translation – with the work of Li Po and Tu Fu, which led to what's been a lifelong commitment to the work of both those poets and to the T'ang Dynasty poets in general. As with Williams, I learned much about brevity and precision, but I especially came to understand the value of the image, and how much work that could do, instead of a lot of words.

But the largest influence is the sentence as handled by a variety of prose writers. In English, the novels of Henry James and George Eliot, the essays of William James, Proust in translation – these writers are responsible for my addiction to the sentence and all of its possibilities; to this day, I'm more interested in the sentence than in the line. Equally important for sentences have been the prose of Tacitus and of Thucydides, both of whom I studied in college, and whom I had intended to do doctoral work on, before I abandoned my doctoral studies. But my plan had been to look at the sentence as a tool for psychological and emotional manipulation and control...

This is really just the tip of the proverbial iceberg. I read constantly, and the influences are constantly shifting. But these are some of the writers whose influence has been the most important for me. There are so many individual writers, especially from the twentieth century and this one, who have been crucial. Frank Bidart, Jorie Graham, Rita Dove, Robert Hayden, Marie Howe, Rose-marie Waldrop, Brigit Pegeen Kelly, Randall Jarrell, Pamela Alexander, Linda Gregg, Jean Valentine, Larry Levis...

Oh! I almost forgot how Geoffrey Hill changed my life when I took a course with him in religious poetry, back in 1992. The course focused only on Christian religion. Until then, I had never read the metaphysical poets – his course included all of those – Donne and Herbert especially, who have been huge influences on my poems, along with Hopkins; the course also included such unlikely poets as Frank O'Hara and Robert Lowell. Southwell. Coleridge. Between that course, and another course I took (I forget the professor's name, though) in Milton, I became fascinated with the Old and New Testaments, which I'd never read or been raised on. I fairly quickly abandoned the New, but the Old Testament fascinated, perhaps in the way that Dante's *Inferno* fascinates more than his *Paradiso* does, for me. There's so much resonance between the Old Testament and Greek Tragedy, I find, that same distance between human impulse and divine (but sometimes societal) expectation. Herbert and Donne especially spoke to me because of how they showed in their poems a resistance to belief, or a struggle towards belief, that feels more authentic to me than an unquestioning faith. I say all of this as a nonbeliever...

A question about doubt. You have written 'we as humans can't resist trying to find solutions'. And you've talked in an earlier answer about feeling 'in between a number of constituencies'. Am I correct in thinking that your poems are often about doubt, and if so, how much of that doubt relates to your own personal situation and how much by what you see around you?

Doubt is definitely a way of thinking of it, yes, though I tend to think of it more as a desire to be precise about things that many people only superficially seem to interrogate. I think it's part of the poet's work to push beneath assumption – maybe this is my version of what Socrates seems to have meant about the examined life? For me, any sentence is a questing forward on the part of imagination, but with an attention to precision or accuracy – which is why, I suppose, the sentences often involve revision, self-correction. To give an example, if I say to someone 'I'll love you until I die', as soon as I say that the question arises: how do I know this to be true? What if this other person becomes monstrous and we're no longer happy – will I love him still? What if I find my own ideas of love have changed, and this person no longer fits what I need or what I can give? So, what seemed a simple enough thing to say is seen, under examination, not to be so simple; and if I'm going to announce endless devotion to a person, I owe it to them, and to myself, to know exactly what I mean, so I *can* mean it. Obviously, this isn't how I think all the time. A reviewer once said that he imagined I couldn't order a taco without going into some metaphysical state of examination! I order tacos all the time, without thinking about it! But tacos aren't love, or desire, or freedom, or death.

And yes, my doubt is very much connected to my personal situation, insofar as I'm a human being and there's so much about being one of those that is messy, unclear – how to be a partner, how to be a citizen, how to know oneself – questions whose answers shift across our entire lives and never get resolved. I feel that being alive as a person at all involves not knowing, much of the time, and trying to understand, and trying to trust, but also realizing that trust can be misplaced, things can be misunderstood – to doubt seems in some ways to be part of survival. But beyond just being a human, I think being marginalized all one's life – because of race and queerness – has meant growing up doubting the status quo that I didn't fit, but meanwhile the power of that status quo can make me doubt myself. Meanwhile, there's the doubt that comes with being old enough to not always remember things – or I remember them, but differently from how others might remember them, which can make me doubt my memory, theirs, memory itself...

About the natural world. You commented at a reading that a friend had said there was 'too much of the natural world in your poems'. Do you think this is true? Has your inclusion of the natural world changed over your writing career and do you have particular influences in terms of portraying the natural world in your poetry?

Well, maybe I misquoted at the time, but what my friend said was he thought I should have more urban material in my poems, given that I live in a city – he wondered why the poems were so full of natural imagery, as if the city didn't exist for me. I disagree with him entirely. Because poems aren't mere transcriptions of what's right in front of us, or they're not that for me. And poems reflect our sensibility, the world we inhabit in our minds, the worlds we carry with us, sometimes by choice, sometimes inevitably. After spending the first fourteen years of my life moving from air force base to air force base, I settled on Cape Cod, in Massachusetts, where I imagined I'd spend the rest of my life. All through high school and college, the sea was part of my daily life, the marshes, the forests; the house my parents bought was in the middle of the woods, which I'd walk through in order to get to the school bus. It makes sense to me that this landscape printed itself on my thinking and has shaped it. The landscape changed when I moved to St. Louis for a job, but after almost thirty years there, I still find that my poems contain a lot of the imagery from where I grew up. But this makes complete sense to me. Willa Cather eventually wrote her novels from New York City, but most of them took place in the Nebraskan prairie where she grew up. Landscape haunts us, defines us, in ways we can't entirely track.

What my friend forgets, though, is that the natural world also exists in cities. I live near a vast park here in St Louis, where I bring my dog most days, and we tend to go to a particular pond that's surrounded by trees; the pond itself has egrets wandering its edges, there's the occasional muskrat. Meanwhile, much of the landscape of my poems comes from my backyard, which has a catalpa tree, a stand of bamboo, an ancient pear tree, a couple dogwoods... yes, past all of that, I can see a couple of high rises, but they aren't what interests me. And why shouldn't our own poems contain what we're interested in?

A question about masculinity. Representations of masculinity are featured in your poems in terms of male relationships but also as authoritative figures such as kings and emperors. Do you feel that there is a kind of 'quest for authenticity' in your representations of masculinity, and what kinds of factors complicate this search?

Hmm, I'm not certain what you mean by a quest for authenticity – authentic masculinity? I don't know if I'd agree that there is such a thing. To speak to the first part of your question, I'd say that my suspecting, at around thirty, that I was gay was the catalyst for my writing poems again after a silence of about seven years. And part of my delay in understanding my queerness was that there weren't any models, that I could find, for how male-male relationships might viably work. So the first book wrestled with that, and the second book, written when I'd entered my first relationship with a man, was very much an investigation into this area. I didn't really think I was writing about masculinity, though, I just wanted to figure out how I could fashion a life for myself in a world whose definitions of a relationship didn't include me. Believe it or not, I didn't even think my poems were homoerotic – I found that out the hard way, when I gave my first few readings and saw how shocked people were by what I'd taken for granted...

But over time, I have grown more interested in how power works in relationships generally, regardless of sex, though it's true that the context for me is always between men, since that's what I know. Early on, I was fascinated with how much emphasis was put, in the gay world, on who was a 'top' or a 'bottom', for example, and how those roles were associated with power and powerlessness, respectively (and incorrectly), when the truth is of course more fluid than that – in my experience, power is ever-shifting, and has to do with so many things, age differences if there are any, differences in financial stability, differences in personality. And while I didn't plan it, I think the presence of kings and emperors might have something to do with how they are emblematic of a certain kind of power. It's also true, though, that my strongest two influences on how I think might be the *Iliad* and *The Lord of the Rings*; the latter is where I spent all of my adolescence, it seems, long before the movie version – I can't say how many times I read those books as a teenager. And the *Iliad* is a touchstone for me, to this day – talk about a book that presents us with a range of masculinities and shows how vulnerability can also be a part of masculinity...

My final question is about contradictions. I mentioned in an earlier review that I saw your poems as containing a sense of isolation, but also a profound acceptance of the human condition. Do you feel that you reach a resolution of contradictions through poetry?

I think my answer might connect with what you've said about a profound acceptance of the human condition (thank you, by the way, for those words!). I think the human condition is by definition contradictory, who we are is in constant flux and revision. Given that, I don't believe it makes sense to try to resolve those contradictions. To resolve suggests there's something wrong that needs to be fixed, somehow. Resolution feels dishonest, to me – lacking in the precision that I spoke of earlier. I see my poems as containers where the contradictions aren't so much resolved as presented faithfully; the containment, though – the poem – gives a temporary sense of stability to the contradictions. They're still swirling around, but a little less randomly than if they hadn't been somewhat tethered by language and given boundaries by form. I've always felt, after writing a poem, that there's been a brief stay to the chaos of being the particular human that I am. The stay is brief, because resolution is false – there's no resolution to the large abstractions that our lives include. But this lack of permanent stability becomes the catalyst for the next poem, each poem a kind of feinting forward, maybe, another attempt or essay, from when essay meant to try, as I suppose it still does... I hope that my poems don't try to resolve the human condition, but to present it honestly – which is indeed an acceptance of that condition, though for me acceptance doesn't mean I don't routinely question it. But I agree with Keats and his negative capability – the poet doesn't seek to resolve the questions but lives among them. This seems a good definition, too, of what it means to be human.

Thanks are due to Livi Michael for additional help with this interview.

Three More Shibari Catulluses

ISOBEL WILLIAMS

4 *Phaselus ille, quem videtis, hospites,*

Oh there was never another to touch her –
Yes, the drinks will be out in a minute –
Broad in the beam all right
But the fastest hull that flew and she knew it,
Flashing her stern at the boy
Racers from Thessaloniki
Under oars or canvas,

All logged here:
The Adriatic coast ('lethal'),
The Cycladēs, your famous Rhodes,
The Sea of Marmara ('vicious north wind'),

The Black Sea shoreline ('horrific')
Where she grew up as trees,
Whispering adolescence with swishy hair,
Toes dug in the earth –
She swore her birth was watched

By pines and rippling box trees
High above Amāstris and Cytōrus –

She would paddle in their shallows
Then floated her master
Through cauldrons of hell
Braced for buffeting from port or starboard
Or borne by even-handed winds of heaven

And never had to pray for safe harbour
From the ultimate sea to this millpond
Where she reminisces
In genteel decay

So pour a libation in her name
To the coxless pair Castor and Pollux

Then we'll go in and chat to the old dears
About the jolly boating weather.

62 *Vesper adest, iuvenes, consurgite: Vesper Olympo*

Vespas vespers passeggiata
Vespertinal bell

Vespertilio *Latin for bat (the mammal)*
Vesta Tilley male impersonator

Vesta goddess of the hearth
Vestal Virgins keepers of the flame
Swan Vestas matches made of aspen

'I trembling like an aspen leaf stood sad and bloodlesse
   quyght.'[1]

Boys:
Starry pinpricks in the dusk
Before our big pricks turn to dust
Time to leave the well-stocked bar
Virgo's high and on her way
Let her hear the wedding chant
That hymen better be real, girl, not from a bow-tied
   Wimpole Street abortionist.

Girls:
Watch the boys. They've made their move.
Get in place, mark your opponent
Under artificial light.
Look how confident they are –
Bunch of Eurovision winners.
Absence of what people imagine a hymen might be like has
   led to assault, imprisonment, murder and suicide.

Boys:
Guys, this isn't in the bag.
Look! That's what you call rehearsing.
They've got focus. We're a mess.
At this rate they deserve to win
So concentrate and mark your woman.
Some girls are born without a noticeable hymen.

Girls:
Evening star, the most sadistic
Searchlight in the sky: you gouge
The daughter from her mother's arms,
Daughter clinging to her mother,
Hand her to some randy lout
Like a general when he's seized the state.

1 Arthur Golding, *Metamorphoses* XIV line 245.

The causes of bleeding in the female are ignorance and clumsiness in the male.

Boys:
Evening star, you shed light on the
Case and ratify the deed
Signed by parents then by husbands.
It's enacted when you rise –
Heaven sets the time to close.
Virginity tests are legal in many jurisdictions. They are unscientific.

Girls:
The evening star has abducted our sister.

<loss>

Boys:
You mark the switch to night security.
Burglars sneak out in the dark
But you apprehend them when you
Flood the sky at dawn. Females
Complain about their bedtime duty
But you know they want it really.
Virginity kits are sold online. Ancients used blood in a fish bladder.

Girls:
In the cloistered garden is a
Hidden flower, safe from flocks and
Ploughing, stroked by breezes, nursed by
Sunlight, fed by rain – the crux of
Stifled longing for boys and girls.
When a sharp nail nips the stalk

No one wants the fallen petals.
Virgin state is loved by all
But if purity is spoiled
Boys lose interest, girls grow cold.
A bride may file a fingernail to a point and cut her thigh so that she bleeds on to the sheet which must be exhibited to her family.

Boys:
Vine neglected on bare field
Never has a ripened yield.
Single state is unforgiving,
Main stem flops and furthest striving
Tendril barely reaches root:
Farmer and beast squash underfoot.

Vine submits to husbandry –
Farmer digs and beast comes by.
If she's not correctly mated
She grows old uncultivated.
Bound to a firm rising trunk
She is money in the bank
Earning interest on her man's respect,
Not a millstone round her father's neck.

Don't go fighting marriage wars,
Girl. Your body isn't yours.
One third is assigned to father,
One more third allowed to mother.
What's left over is for you
So you're one share against two.
During the service they transfer
Theirs to the groom so call him sir.
*'Honour, high honour and renown,
To Hymen, god of every town!'*[2]

2 Shakespeare, *As You Like It*.

67 *O dulci iucunda viro, iucunda parenti,*

*What's in and out and banging?
A door!*

*No, I wouldn't say I trivialised things,
Quite the opposite*

*So here's the dream – with lots of my specials:
Betrayal, genitalia, towers, vegetables,
My home town, urination, virgins and money.
All that's missing is the mule.*

No, not her, I mean an actual mule.

Now, what's more reassuring to a
Nice bland hubby and his bride's parents than –
Oh hello, stout front door with a good thick bolt.
May the freeholder grant you a nice lick of varnish.
I hear you kept it shut for old man Balbus
When he lived here,

But you came unhinged
Once he was laid out on the slab and his heir
Moved in with the new wife.

Then Door lets in a draught of words –
An entrance entranced with itself:

'Not guilty, with all due respect to the present owner,
Although every time there's bother
The riffraff call out, "Door, it's all your fault."'

Your word against theirs. Can you make it stand up?

'How? No one cares.'

(Door needs oiling.) Oh yes we do.

'Well, that stuff about her being carried
Over my threshold a virgin is balls.

Her first husband didn't touch her
With that appendage which never reached an acute
Angle (wilted chard was harder),
But to ruin the unhappy home
His dad scored a hole in one –
Either he couldn't control his disgusting urges
Or the son was gelded
And someone had to whip out a length of gristle
To get her clothes off and continue the line.'

Yeah you're wearing your 'romance is dead' look
But that's what I put in my dream diary word for word
So I'll carry on if you don't mind.

I say to Door:
What a great example of paternal devotion
To piss through his son's keyhole.

Door runs with the theme:
'The gentle golden stream flows by the banks of

Brescia under the watchtower – a desirable
Location which gave rise to my own dear Verona –
And it was on Brescia CCTV
That she opened her letterbox to Postumius.
And Cornelius.

Some may ask, in between knob jokes,
How I'm wise to the action, being a fixture?
Well, I've listened in to her furtive whispers
With the domestics – she thinks I'm a block of wood.
And there's another notch on her bedpost
But if I name him he'll give me a hammering.
Ginger. Tall. Got sued in a
High-rolling false paternity case.'

And I've worked out who it is.
Obvious. Go on, guess.
Oh sorry, I didn't notice the time.
I'll think of a good knock-knock gag for next week.

To Ludwig Wittgenstein

FREDERIC RAPHAEL

'W.', in the vocative, best serves to summon and summarise your mythical personality. In 1951, when I was first intrigued by Moral Sciences – as Cambridge formality (following David Hume) then termed philosophy – you had just left the scene, messiah whose apostles took him to have relegated metaphysics to the old curiosity shop. I was a callow twenty-year-old, apt with parodic proses and verses in Latin and Greek, bent on fiction, hot for the exit of ideology, including religion. The end of the war had seemed to promise a freshly levelled playing field. You were cast as Reason's referee, decisive with the whistle at any flash of supposititious fancy. I took Freddie Ayer, author of the razor-edged *Language, Truth and Logic,* to be your linesman.

You had been barely twenty in 1911, when Bertrand Russell was approached, in Trinity, by a shriven Germanic pilgrim and, pretty soon, disconcerted by him. G.E. Moore suspected your rare quality when you alone looked puzzled in his lectures. Not long afterwards, the author of *Principia Ethica,* Bloomsbury's secular gospel, went with you on a Norwegian retreat on which he, a full professor, played your *amanuensis.* What other incursion into Britannia's philosophical élite has matched yours for disruptive intensity? I read you as possessed with passion for once and for all truthfulness, the stripping out of fancy. Philosophy, you said later, 'leaves everything as it is'; but you left philosophy quite other than it had been (Bertrand Russell too).

Displacement of morals and ethics in favour of engi-

neering, aeronautics and the totalitarian dream presaged the Great War; mechanical progress pandered to press-button ruthlessness, mark of the twentieth century. You did your duty in the Austro-Hungarian army but took no loud pride in it. Was there a pinch of insolence in volunteering for that solitary steeple-high perch – close to the Cross? – from which to co-ordinate artillery fire on enemies with whom you had no quarrel? Your entry in *Zettel* for Christmas Day 1916, when you may have been up there on duty, jingles no bells. Higher mathematics ignores holy days. In logic there are no surprises, you said, and no God – I took you to imply – to spring them. Then again a suicidal strain ran through the Wittgensteins and marked a blaze it would be coy not to link with Semitic origins; self-denial can be self-destruction's double. We shall, as academics say, come back to that.

Calamity for the Central Powers and its ruling houses dashed the patriotic vanity you might have scorned, had the double eagle not been cropped of one of its hawkish heads. Your pianist brother Paul lost an arm, Austria lost Hungary; the Wittgenstein fortune emerged intact. Post-Versailles, you left no longer imperial Vienna and returned to Cambridge, as if after a sabbatical, to say 'Where were we?' When it came to qualifying for the PhD, necessary to academic advancement, Moore and Russell sat as examiners you chose to patronise. 'You'll never understand it' you told them about your thesis, joker trumping aces. Did any other such submission ever resemble the *Tractatus Logico-Philosophicus*? No sooner was it construed as a work of genius than its composer discounted it. Your programme for a language congruent with a reasonable world was a post-Armistice casualty of the Great War. Common decency died of wounds. The Jabberwocky came, left and right, in the wake of the old order.

Whatever your second thoughts, the *Tractatus* was seminal in post-Versailles Vienna; philosophical *klatches* prowled and prowled around your numbered bastion. Deserted by its architect, impregnable and defenceless, it resembled that castellated octagon built in Apulia by Friedrich II von Hohenzollern. Did you ever sight-see? What fails to interest genius is always interesting. Did you whistle while you worked, or only afterwards, or before, at faultless length, one-man orchestra? Playing your clarinet, were you ever tempted to jazz? You seem, in biographies, as austere as that centimetre-perfect steel and glass house I visited in Vienna's Kundmanngasse; no place like home, as they say, no place whatever in that instance. You helped Paul Engelmann engineer it for your sister when in retreat from a petty reverse. See below; Freud's place to look.

Translated to 1930s England, you came to accept a Cambridge professorship, with small gratitude, even less collegiate zeal. You offered no welcome to 'tourists' at those seminarian huddles in your rooms in Whewell's Court, across from the Taj Mahal restaurant where 1950s Johnians clustered over three-and-sixpenny curries. Celebrity-hunters were advised to knock on other oaks than yours. Like Archilochus' hedgehog, you bristled with singularity. Did adroit Isaiah, Berlin that is, ticket you in that uncuddly form, himself the versatile fox? As if scorched by your unaccommodating heat, Berlin abandoned philosophising in favour of *recyclage,* black coat, striped trousers, carnation buttonhole, rich wife: metic as local toff, the first Jew to have been elected a Fellow of All Souls, the English language his neatly buttoned carapace.

Unlike the devil, you had no nickname. Disciples furnished a pedestal for your five feet, six inches. Didactic solipsist, archetypal one-off, 'Wittgenstein' branded the ladder you supplied for trammelled escapees from the metaphysical fly-bottle; once out, they would be wise, you said, to fling it away. Philosophy had no heights to scale, no lofty furniture, no celestial rewards. When Pompey the Great invaded the temple in Jerusalem in 63 B.C. and unveiled the Holy of Holies, its lack of treasure left him robbed. Vacancy was content; zero a mystery the Romans never plumbed. Latter-day Spinoza, you ground metaphorical lenses the more clearly to see less and less.

Russell was sometimes called Bertie, behind his back, by undergraduate Moral Scientists of my time. I attended his last series of lectures. So many people came to the first that the overflow overflowed, into Mill Lane. Russell declared that he suspected that many had come 'for the wrong reasons'. 'Accordingly' subsequent lectures would be 'more difficult'. Uncomfortable was he, the mandarin, with the popularity he had helped to publicise? Or proud? You had your secret apprehension; did he have his? Imagination was not your field, unless dread, cousin to menace, was its crop: scourge and fruit confounded. The

nearest you came to self-revelation was in that paradigm hybrid, the rabbit and the duck; Jew and Gentile, as you never said, in an Orwellian farmyard, Napoleon and Snowball. Freddie Ayer wondered whether or what sheep were thinking. His master, Gilbert Ryle, affected to discount 'mind' altogether. You spoke or did not speak. Did your silences ever lose their foreign accent?

Ayer, for all his wartime Guards' officer rig, Old Etonian tie, and knightly embellishments, dreaded that one day they might come for him, another *Jud Süss*. Bluebeard's castle loomed; Kafka's too; and *The Trial*? A palace and a prison on either hand, Freddie's nimble-mindedness wore a secret ball and chain. Had he not said so, who would have guessed? Because he said so, was it true? Even apprehensions can be self-important. Something is missing in all biographies; otherwise they would be lives. It was said, in my days as a *habitué* at parties at 5, Jordan's Yard, that there was a knock at the door on one such occasion and, when some lit *au pair* girl opened it, a grey head craved entrance. She took a look and said, 'Old people's home is number eleven' and shut the door, on Bertrand Russell, *dit-on.* There is a nine of diamonds in every suit.

However straight your face, or aghast John Wisdom's, you and he treated philosophy as a litter of often insoluble cryptograms rather than as any coherent system; disassembly was the way to make its elements intelligible. You came to call philosophising 'the game', as whores their activities. In Attic drama, the same *topos* could accommodate solemnity and frivolity. 'The modal child, Wisdom used to say, "is the child around whom the others cluster".' If ethics are equated with aesthetics, as you bracketed them in the *Tractatus,* your dictum entailed that Leni Riefenstahl's 1935 *Triumph of the Will,* glorifying a Nazi rally, was beyond criticism; beauty its goodness. Might that dispose you to think again about that slick equation?

Logic has something in common with Talos, the hot-chested, tireless Cretan automaton invented by the crafty Daedalus; any intrusive exception, clapped against the grill where it might have had a heart, was toast. As the Jews of Europe were being consigned to extinction, Heinrich Himmler (another one-time schoolteacher) asked a blonde, naked, beautiful Jewess merely to swear that she was not Jewish. He could then spare her the gas chamber. The twentieth century's anonymous Antigone denied him the divine right, died for what she was. So? So suppose that you had surrendered your family's tons of bullion to save her life, as you did for your sisters' sake, never mind that it armed the Nazis. Would that blonde Antigone not have looked at you with contempt? After Auschwitz, you played the British game: reticence muzzled the unspeakable. You quizzed, but did you ever embarrass, yourself included? Fencing goes around the minefield, never ventures inside, protects what those skulls and crossbones warn against. Philosophers also fence; thieves too their stolen valuables.

Your notion of repairing to the USSR stands as one of the few callow moments in your life. Lenin, in his Zurich days, had propounded dialectical materialism as a doctrine that denounced the Vienna Circle's polemic neutrality. However briefly, you bought Soviet communism, the prospectus if not the savage practice, quite as if the old world and its suite of clerics, *rentiers* and hypocrites deserved eclipse, never mind the conduct of its ravenous replacement. That 1935 visit of yours to the Soviet Union coincided with the beginning of the Great Terror, whereof, so far as I know, you kept silent, as you did, when the time came, about the Holocaust and the logics applied to sanctify inhumanity. Not your field? I took you for the moral authority I craved and you never affected to be.

How did you see, or not see, yourself? In Greek iconography, only women look in mirrors. Are human beings not sometimes perceived more accurately by other people than by themselves? My daughter Sarah, when asked to paint a portrait of the retiring Master of Jesus College, Cambridge, suggested to him that she first do a drawing. 'To be sure that you can get a likeness, you mean?' 'No,' Sarah said, 'So that you can see what you look like.' Lewis Namier, in the Athenaeum, asked politely how he was, responded, 'Am I a physician?' He shared your *morgue*; ironic masks are common among scholars.

Austria-Hungary's post-Versailles dissection docked a measure of the pride that came from deleting yourself from the gilded order your family enjoyed. How else shall we read your decision to secede from metropolitan wrangling, and play schoolteacher in a mountain village? Your intolerance of error was not effaced. Pupils responsive to your urgent teaching made remarkable progress. Inattentive ears were boxed hard enough to excite rustic indignation. Disdaining to be chided, you returned to Vienna to work on your sister's house. Before long, the lure of philosophising at the centre table uncorked your bottle. Can you deny that the dated expression has fizzy pertinence? Discussion has violent roots: *discutere* to shake apart. You resumed bending first-class ears while what was left of Austria came unglued. Oh yes, another pun lurks, brutal and artless.

The oddest *fait divers* in your life was having been in adjacent classes with little Adolf Hitler when in primary school at Linz. Was he Adolf Schickelgruber then? Did anyone box his ears, or yours? The former is easier to imagine; it happened or it didn't. Another nine of diamonds! You became solipsists of opposing orders, rant and reason, urgent to prevail, dictators literal and figurative. Imagine if... Never mind. Did you hear the story about Bob Boothby, a maverick Scottish Tory MP, a regular in high and low circles, when some time in the 1930s, he was presented to Adolf Hitler? The Führer greeted him with his selfish upraised arm and 'Heil Hitler'. Boothby replied, with similarly upraised arm, 'Heil, Boothby!' Humour has little place in philosophy. Democritus saw the funny side, but it was not catching. In speculative verbosity, are the dancer and the dance ever one?

Being 'difficult' was not your mark, not during your Second Coming anyway; uncompromising, yes. The story goes that you were once approached by a lady who said she had a problem: she did not feel at home in the universe. You are said to have said, 'That, madam, is not a problem, it is a difficulty', implying 'next window, please'. Freud might have helped her; you not. Russell had a similar experience with a lady who maintained that the earth was flat and sustained on the back of a gigantic tortoise. Russell inquired nicely on what the tortoise reposed. 'Another giant tortoise; as far as we're concerned it's tortoises, tortoises all the way.'

Odd that the method still ascribed to your mature self is termed 'therapeutic positivism'. Is it therapy? Is it positivism? Their seen-through ghost? It is not the answers that come at the end of your book, but the questions. The crux of philosophy: it never supplies what we want, unless a charlatan propounds it. Difficulty doesn't make anything true; the clever wish it did: why else did George Steiner fawn on Heidegger? The hope of being admitted as exceptional to the Aryan rule, as Alan Ginsburg with Ezra Pound? Your name was neither mocked nor abbreviated, despite faecal possibilities; no Nietzsche, no feature rhymed with you; what would it be to falsify, trade on, pervert, toy with your thought? Made curricular, it furnished tracks, and points, for trains carrying aseptic cargo, powerless engines. I met a man recently who affected to be a philosopher as well as a publisher. He said he had no time for you. That was his right. He turned out to be a con man.

Is there any recording of your Cambridge seminars? You uttered no Joadian catchphrases; only your gestures – bracketing sidelong hands, advancing or retreating, boxing clever, it seemed – were cadged by latter-day apostles who affected the arcane fellowship which select disciples had enjoyed in your presence. Your manual code composed a waggish semaphore; caution primed distinctions, straitened gates; your scowl a shutter: poor Friedrich Waismann, common ground his trespass! Possessiveness did not vanish with possessions, did it?

Did you ever value despatches that saluted you? Some people take praise for insolence, save no welcome for men from Porlock. Isolation prompts outspokenness, prison liberties: Boethius, Sir Walter Raleigh, Antonio Gramsci. When did Leopardi and Montaigne have more to say than on their own? Solipsism and egotism are not the same thing. Contrast your parable of the man who read something in the newspaper and then went out and bought another copy of the same paper to verify its truth. Imagine having nothing to lose; is that what impelled you to give away your share of the Wittgenstein fortune?

There was at least one thing of which you never divested yourself: nettled respect for Otto Weininger, the raw rash he raised. Carlo Michelstadt, another suicide at twenty-three, enough said, did you ever find time for him? Consider rhetoric and its false floor, Trieste and *tristesse*, spectrum and spectre, fostering Claudio Magris and the biggest synagogue in Europe. Shucking Jewishness can narrow horizons without erasing its mark. Why else did you label the philosopher a solitary without a place to call his own; sly reference to the Son of Man, was it? Windowless monad, ghetto for one, bare bed of *nihilismo,* are they not elements of what Julien Benda celebrated in *Exercice d'un enterré vif*? *Vif* suggests *Juif, n'est-ce pas*? Silences pun in different languages.

By the time you took up permanent residence in Cambridge, Russell's singlemindedness had dissipated. His public renown came from popular texts on morals (one advocating 'experimental marriage') which you held should be clapped in red jackets to advertise their unworthiness. Blue would distinguish works rated (by you) as having intellectual merit. Diffidence outgrown, you were the master now. Did Russell ever honour you more unequivocally than by omitting any mention of you in *A History of Western Philosophy*? Did you ever rate, or berate, Heidegger, whose metaphysics furnished absurdities for the Vienna Circle's lighter moments? Heidegger's brother read him for a solemn Dadaist. Reichsmarshall Hermann Goering's brother helped to smuggle Jews into Switzerland. Saint or seditious sibling? Both? What would it be to know the answer? Decision may classify; it is not a form of knowledge.

That deckchair in which you sat during Cambridge seminars furnished a canvas throne, as Diogenes' tub his palace. When young you were racked by what Russell called your sins and by their purge: dread of not measuring up to your ambition to be a philosopher, was that? Or of 'something coming out', as they used to say? Is motive ever only one thing? No such thing as the self, John Gray claims in one of his buy-me pamphlets; self-preservation is there though, anything but still, scissors and pasting against the odds, dressing the void. Only the soul has no colour. When you proclaimed that philosophy lacked exclusive authority, you docked the once 'Queen of Sciences' of its regal coat of arms. At the same time, warning apprentices against its glitter conceded its lure. As you wound things up, you restored their tick.

Whatever you may have confessed, or given away, ducking or rabbiting, there were elements you kept to yourself, unless you deceived yourself as well as those who took you for a 'Christian' and proposed, as the Geaches did, to bury you with a cross marking the spot. Thanks to them, was it, that you have a headstone in Cambridge's Ascension parish church? Your *Tractatus*, mantic and misconceived, as you concluded, posted Baruch Spinoza, Russell's 'noblest of philosophers', as your nominal cousin, Benedict. The convert lives more comfortably in translation than in the original.

Weininger's shamelessness made a trimmer out of you, did it not? Were you a little ashamed to discount him merely because he was wrong? You dared to say that his work expressed 'a great truth' provided one preceded it with Russell's wavering dash, which symbolised negation. Did that not all but concede that being correct, formally, is never everything; the rub, the rub? Weininger discussed matters from which, unlike physical danger, you chose to absent yourself. His sense of cloven predestination, like the synthetic *a priori,* was not rational. It remained lethal; Christian stigma led to selection; goats this way, sheep that. Detach divinity, stigmata stick.

That first visit of yours to Cambridge, before the Great War, to sit at Russell's feet, before snapping at his heels, had a licensing effect; so Jesus when endorsed by John the Baptist, Eliot when Pounded. Apollo warned against the oracle over which he presided: *gnothi seauton* implied the futility of looking other than within for the truth about oneself; within what? The sign over Dante's hell was matched over Auschwitz. During the long calvary of European Jewry, you absented yourself from Cambridge to become a hospital orderly in Newcastle. War work

allowed you to be yourself, unless it was someone else.

William Bartley III's account of your younger days alleges that you had indulged yourself with the 'rough trade' available in Vienna's Leopoldstadt park, implying that Newcastle had similar pleasures available. He has been accused of muck-raking, yet he was, in other regards, a respectable philosopher. What impelled him to spill wanton beans, what source delivered them? Renan's *Vie de Jésus* was regarded as scandalous in its day, because – like Thucydides – it eliminated the supernatural. Bartley's Wittgenstein revelled in the liberties of wartime obscurity. If true, does whatever you were alleged to have got up or down to damage your integrity? For all your interest in Freud, you never played the moralist; what individuals chose to do, or found they dreamed about, was their affair. I wonder what you would have made of D.H. Lawrence, he of you. Better than he did of Russell? Lady Ottoline Morell, absurd as she may now appear, had unnerving effects on all three of you. There's a topic.

Once anointed a philosopher by Russell, you began a long parade of detachment and disdain. Your conceit declared itself in that parenthetic exit line, after you and Popper indulged in a retrospective Viennese coffee-house barney, in the Cambridge Moral Sciences Club, in October 1946. The grandee and the prodigy in you banged the door on your exit line: 'What do you know about philosophy, Russell, what have you ever known?' Michelangelo Antonioni was given to not calling 'cut' when the actors expected it. He let the camera run when the scene, as scripted was over. Then the truth would show up, he hoped, for want of confected words. Actors, he imagined, looked more true in a panic void. Would that some angelic vigilante could deliver footage of you going down the steps from Richard Braithwaite's rooms into the courtyard! How did you look, where? How did you walk? At what angle was your chin? Popper's *The Open Society and Its Enemies* has proved durably canonic. Although most reputable sources do not quote your exit line, it has a plausible ring: Russell had omitted any mention of you in his recently published and popular *History of Western Philosophy*. We may be sure you would have had it bound in red.

From the beginning, your pronouncements had a stinging effect on Russell. How much pleasure did you take when demonstrating to him, in the last days of Edwardian Britain's complacent *imperium*, that his (and Alfred North Whitehead's) long attempt to make mathematics the basis of transcendental knowledge amounted to a Jacob's ladder horizontal with elaborated tautologies: the end no higher than the beginning. Russell had the nobility to honour your dismissive rigour; that does not promise that he forgave it. Logic makes few friends. Some say Russell never again did work of fundamental importance in philosophy. A fierce disciple might say that there was no such work to be done; would you, wholeheartedly? Delete the fraudulent, the fictional, the dramatic, the practically meaningless, who can argue, or deny, that writing remains on the wall, invisible or no? The unnecessary (logically) can still, and often, make humans wear and bear their stripes and stars. Is that Jean-Jacques Rousseau's point? Was he right? Shall we ask Voltaire? Philosophers compete, ruthlessly, for a crown with no known kingdom. They also do their share of careerist crawling. Forty percent of German academics heiled Hitler.

Empiricism's puzzle: why must it be logically unavoidable and practically absurd to be only as we are? I Am That I Am: God's boast or His lament? 'Why not?' trumps 'Why?' as fundamental. Hence G.E. Moore took your puzzlement for a symptom of rare intelligence? Jesus did not spring God from His loneliness; never a Christian, He was tagged as one; seal of Roman imperialism, universal deity posed as irreplaceable. No wonder Plato, faker and fakir, was embraced as Christianity's adjutant! Was Jesus ever tempted to make a getaway, once on earth, from celestial bloodlessness? Is that what the devil was up to during that dialogue on the pinnacle of the temple, displaying the sweets of here and now? Suppose, as D.H. Lawrence fancied, Jesus dreamed of shedding divinity, finding sweet mutability in being uncapitalised he, the son a father. No such luck? *Moira* lives, *Tyche*'s plain sister.

John Locke's plausible claim that the human mind was a *tabula rasa,* ready for education's scratches, served to warrant universal suffrage, falsely: DNA, no sort of leveller, pitches humanity into a hazardous mixer, irrational desire the whisk. Nice that DNA's discoverers were laurelled shoplifters, Watson and Crick; some of the jewels in their Nobel crown were filched from Rosalind Franklin. I once saw a sign in a Madison Avenue costumier's window: 'Everything in this store is guaranteed fake.' The Cretan question: including the sign? The Cretan's Paradox can never be the Cretan's to resolve; it can only be put to him; and then he cannot answer it; neither truthfully nor falsely. So what? The potter pots until he elects to do no more; the work detached from his wheel, however sweetly, has its navel, mark of its human source; done and dusted is never immaculate. No work of art is ever finished, they say, only abandoned, like hope.

Your return to Cambridge, ten years after the Armistice, was sometimes referred to, if not in your hearing, as 'the Second Coming'. In every class there has to be a naughty boy. You published no New Testament to supplement or disavow the *Tractatus.* The circulation of the manuscript blue and green notebooks made your apocrypha available, on loan, to warranted insiders. 'Not many laughs there, dear', John Schlesinger might have said: has anyone a record of your laughing at anything anyone said? Your warmest acknowledgment, one guesses, was a frown. We can be sure only that you were scornful when it came to sentimental assumptions. After Norman Malcolm, your American (significant?) buddy, claimed that assassinating Hitler would be contrary to the British character, you derided the idea that there was any subterfuge, or shortcut, from which the British were too fine, by definition, to abstain. Maurice Buckmaster told me that, during the war, the British launched seemingly shipwrecked boxes to drift ashore in occupied France containing large size condoms, labelled SMALL. Good one? Ian Fleming's idea? Who he? You're probably right.

The notion of national characteristics touched on matters you usually chose not to broach. How good was your English? Part of your rare reputation depended on the Sibylline delivery with which we were quick to bless you. It is not unusual for aliens revered by Englishmen as masters of literary profundity (Conrad by Russell, for instance) to lack conversational fluency. The great classical scholars never affected to *speak* Greek or Latin. Eduard Frankel's edition of Aeschylus is a scholarly masterpiece and a translation into gobbledegook. If German backed your mental agility, you elected to limit your thoughts to a quite specific field; Betty Grable's nimble charms on the sunset side of it, 'Can you do a flick?' your slang proposal when her legs were on a local screen. I remember a German on our Greek beach stopping to say 'I'fe got a bum knee.' Characteristic of German speakers, fluency that promises lumpen foreignness?

Casimir Lewy was a Cambridge philosopher of your period and – unlike you, the anticipator – an all but just in time refugee. When Anthony Rudolf thought of becoming a Moral Scientist, Lewy told him to go away and read, among other books, René Descartes' *Discours de la méthode,* but not in French: an English translation would lack seductive garlic. Tutored by Wisdom, Lewy had become a logician who stayed in his lane. Formal logic supplied the fence over which he could pitch rotten apples, but never reach for good. Far-fetched doubletalk? Cf. skid-marks, their silent screech. Did Lewy write, say, *feel,* anything about what came to be indexed under *The Holocaust?* Wasn't there a clerihew 'What Dr Ewing/ claimed to be doing/ was a load of hooey/ said Casimir Lewy'? There is now; what whitewashed wall long lacks writing on it? Logical possibility warrants ruthlessness. Once the premises are in place, and the lather, Occam's razor knows no pity. What Socrates knew: you never know.

You too questioned doctrine, impersonated quizzical procedure. 'A thing is what it is,' Bishop Butler said, 'and not another thing.' Or so we wish; if we do. Can life go on without double-dealing? Nice that bishops' headdress has a cleft in it! Your later work, akin (you implied) to psychiatry, was devoted to unravelling vexed complexities; dissolving knots, spinning out clear threads; thin stuff, some say. Oh that rabbit and that duck! Nursery analogy – Donald Duck, old Mrs Rabbit – bring Disney and Beatrix Potter into the index. You played the oracle from which neither instruction nor prediction could be expected. Philosophy became a training ground for an austere caucus race; none are promised prizes.

John Wisdom was disposed to a kind of larkiness; unlikely that he learned it from you; perhaps it taught you an English you never spoke. Did your acolytes Miss Anscombe and the sockless Peter Geach ever set the table on a roar? The seriousness with which you are so often credited, your disdain for the much-too-niceties of the High Table, suggests you had no time for donnish distractions, but who knows what pleasure you took in the impersonation of uniqueness? How apt that you were a flawless one-man bandsman, able to whistle all the parts in your selection of Brahms, Beethoven and who all else. Mahler? You filled a private auditorium with the ensemble of yourself.

Can a genuine article ring false, a false ring true? Weininger jumps back into the frame, the dreaded – because undisguised and unblinking – Other who recognised in you, *for you*, what your own mirror was cleverly enough cracked not to deliver full face. You thought to shuck yourself of what, later at least, you saw to be what, in essence, you could not dodge. How am I so sure? Because your philosophy, as Cambridge marketed it, promised escape from specificity, the triumph of choice. The philosopher claims, again and again, to serve only, especially, Christianity's substitute, truth without a mythology or a saviour; yet even you, like Descartes and who all else, grew pettish when others (yes, including your honest acolyte Friedrich Waismann) appropriated ideas which, in texts or lectures which delivered them, were paraded as common knowledge. Can truth have an owner? The bourgeois proprietor caught *in flagrante delicto,* were you, on occasion? When you gave away your money, you gave yourself away, or so you hoped; duplicity nodded, Butler blinked.

Your claim, mimicked by John Wisdom, not to have read many curricular philosophers, seems less modest than a promise of originality. Byron said he had never read Shakespeare. I have only recently come across the work, in translation, of Georg Simmel. Did you ever? I was struck by the confident erudition and decorous outspokenness of a Jewish philosopher who suffered the usual malice in Wilhelmine academic circles but seemed to accept them as little more than an irritation. What is remarkable is the freedom with which Simmel drew attention to money as an ingredient to be reckoned with in human ethology. Before you used the cute image of the rabbit and the duck, Simmel argued for the impossibility of pinning down a comprehensive analysis of the human condition; there was no escaping a variety of readings on different scales, a theme germane to the uncertainties declared by Heisenberg, following Heraclitus's *panta rei,* everything is on the move.

Your renunciation of wealth calls for, or rather generates, a more subtle account of the contingent of motives that induced it. After washing your hands of lucre, you considered emigration to the Soviet Union. You went on a visit just before the Great Terror, but not before the diabolisation of Trotsky, *né* Bronstein, and the murderous onset of Stalinist antisemitism. Did you suppose that a penniless penitent would be easily assimilated? Had you offered Stalin your fortune, you might have been welcome, for a while. What else could he want of you? Were you surrendering yourself in order to be a registered nobody, Odysseus' other? Bertrand Russell had been one of the first westerners keen enough to be appalled by the vindictive Vladimir Ilyich when he gloated over the execution of hundreds (soon thousands and thousands) of alleged impediments to the inevitable classless society. How could you have missed the bloodstained decks of the latter-day Potemkin's ship of state? Why were so many German philosophers recruited to antisemitism and so few historians (Mommsen, however 'fascistic', despised Treitschke and company)? Did that question ever interest or perplex you?

In the 1950s, we believed that you had written the last chapter in western *philo*. Implicit in what passed for agnosticism was hope for what could not be specified: retreat of a questionable deity from miraculous influence on human affairs. Spinoza made logic do something similar when he equated nature and the divine. If a negative could not be proved, might its subject be deemed irrelevant without anyone having to say so? Thanks or no thanks to you, this is what my twenty-year-old self imagined philosophy to establish or at least concede. Does the self age, do souls? Impossible, surely. As you lay dying, the story is, Mrs Bevan came in and said that you had visitors. This prompted your last recorded words, 'Tell them I've had a wonderful life'. Did saying so mean you meant it? Or, knowing the credulity of your mourners, was it the solipsist's last laugh? Can it be that all the public events of your lifetime, the horror, the horror, left you unaffected? Death, you said, in the *Tractatus,* 'is not an event of life, it is not lived through'. Whereof one cannot speak, much remains to be said.

Yours sincerely, F.

I Wake Up and other poems

JOHN MUCKLE

I Wake Up

I wake up every morning thinking of you
And your family, bringing joy & hope
Where before there was sadness & despair
Thinking of the great battles of our time
To give everyone a fair shot, a fair shot
That's all we're asking for, all anyone
Is asking for, an end to dreams deferred.

Our better angels put our demons to bed
On eagles' wings, in the palm of God's hand
The moral arc of a story is bent to justice
Blazes across night sky in fiery healing
Standing on shoulders of the generations
Of women & men believing in possibility
Addressing the most difficult questions

In good faith that history has posed for us
Our answers better be good ones this time
Ready for the main performance on the lawn
& the bridesmaids will surround us in white
Incandescence & in their long satin gowns

Singing glory glory to our great nation
Reborn now in the spirit and in the flesh

At last washed clean in rivers of Canaan
I left my hat in San Bernadino, my car's
In the wash to slosh the dents and ashes off
With pressurized water and soap (a long
Revolving yellow mop comes down on top.)
I'm not saying this to annoy you but just
Letting you know I'm thinking good thoughts

& your family out beyond fireball lightning
That balmy evening we celebrated victory
Rolling across the heavens like great marbles
Carried away as the victorious often are
By the moment their rhetoric comes true
Reeling through you as a rehearsal dream
& the week opens its chasm in your heart

There Ain't No Justice

Don't worry too much about the sociology,
An early novella by Herman Hesse will do you.
Once they get you down in the working-class
There's nothing left against which to rebel.
You might as well drown yourself by lying
On the riverbank, head down in a fast-flowing stream
For all anyone will care about you. A terrible
Example, mentioned once, quickly forgotten
For fear of damaging the vulnerable children.

Instead do your homework, keep your head
In the study position, do not meet their eyes
Unless asked, then shine forth with utter devotion.
Follow whatever path they seem to propose.
Nowadays we can punch our way out of paper bags

Important to seize opportunities as they arise
Until you reach majority & nobody's getting paid.
Eventually there's Feltham, a rite of passage.
It's a place where you can turn your life about,
Plough a deeper groove in one you've made.

I'll fight to avenge the death of my sister
Still carrying her rabbit's foot charm, to the end
The choice is always yours, always options
Are held before you like pre-loaded weapons
As if there's anything to work up to or down.
Life is a package pressed into your hands
& you must carry it just as far as you're able.

Essentially

We sail under cloudy skies, distant traffic
Where recently there was none, just bare streets,
Swapping books with a neighbour you never see
Picking up bits of knowledge from a communal skip,
Scrolling the homeopapes for platinum flecks.

I'm working at a new secondary school in Essen.
Bringing you news of this now I'm in the mood.
How to describe such an historical, interesting place?
Words sometimes fail me. Sweetheart, I won't pretend,
Without my phone, I'd just rhyme it with messin'.

Over Essen what you took for enemy fireworks
Were Lancasters, exploding in mid-air, fully loaded,
A blinding purple flare eliminated unlucky seven;
Losses up to sixty per cent, gone up into the ether.
Incidents drift away. But you can't help remembering.

A white elephant sale of memories. Is that racist?
No, but pouring flour into a schoolgirl's handbag is
In case she wants to be white, not only in Essen.

A monument's needed for something they never do.
We have to imagine a new form for such a thing.

Nothing you have said to me makes any true sense
Or, perhaps it does, that's why I replay the parts.
Every scene went by, clawed back repeatedly.
Modes of remorse came to predominate, nostalgia
Being a word I never used, will always regret.

Essentials continue to be essentialized in Essen.
Once armaments, we're now part of a wider culture.
Children flock in trustingly, so pleased to be back
At school, part of a community they will remember
All their lives, whether or not that means anything.

School dinner is always worse than you imagined.
If only we could push the curriculum to one side
Of our plates, these discarded poetry bits & pieces
Turkey twizzlers of a discredited colonial system.
Let's agree to differ if you like, I'll make amends.

Nuash Sabah in conversation

RORY WATERMAN

RW: What encouraged you to start Poetry Birmingham *in 2019? And why the geographical focus, at least in the name?*

NS: I think people who start things, as well as having some intense creative impulse, have some shared quality of restlessness and dissatisfaction with the way things are, so decide to pull up their sleeves and make anew. I was in my second year of a part-time MA at Birmingham City University and would read *PN Review* and *The Poetry Review*; I'd flick through *Poetry London* and *Poetry Wales* at the library, or *The North* whenever I came across it, and feel an appropriate sense of Brummie indignation that the second city didn't have anything like them. I knew of *Bare Fiction* and *Ad Alta,* both linked to the University of Birmingham, but one had ceased to publish, the other was academic, and neither was dedicated specifically to poetry. So, the name was born with the idea really: I wanted there to be a Birmingham poetry magazine and talked my friends into making it with me. I suppose it was also a way of finding my place in contemporary poetry – by creating it.

What 'dissatisfaction with the way things are', other than

the erstwhile absence of a Birmingham-based poetry magazine? How has starting one helped you to 'find your place in contemporary poetry'?

Poetry subculture seemed like a closed, highly incestuous network, heavily weighted towards young, London poets or academics. In Birmingham, there is a thriving scene of poetry nights but the dominant form seemed to be spoken word which was decidedly not my thing and open mics which I had no patience for nor interest in. In both cases, it seemed one of the key things was being part of a clique or 'community' – I just wanted to read and write in the little time I had; I had responsibilities that precluded me from swimming in the social soup of poetry. Besides my lecturer on the MA, I knew no one who was a published poet or involved in publishing and could see no one from my sort of background on any of the important lists. I felt like I couldn't access any of the opportunities or platforms that existed, and I didn't want to waste my time sending out work methodically and waiting six to eight months only to be rejected. Starting up something new seemed more proactive and empowering. *Poetry Birmingham Literary Journal* (*PBLJ*) solicited no poems when we started and even now mainly publishes from open submissions. I'd rather a big poem than a big name. I'd rather spend time doing developmental edits with a new writer in Birmingham who's never been published before than emblazon my covers with the names of Forward Prize-winners who'll be published everywhere anyway. Of course, over a year and a half on from our first issue, I find myself implicated in the closed, highly incestuous network, and am having to manage conflicts of interest.

Why do you call it a 'closed, highly incestuous network'? You make it sound as though you'd rather do something else.

I love editing the magazine, though it was an incidental pathway that grew out of trying to navigate publishing as an aspiring writer. Commissioning and editing is quite nerdy in a way that I find engaging and fun – I'm thinking of the nitty-gritty quotidian tasks of researching books and poets, playing with ideas for features, tinkering with sentences and lines, typography software, manuscripts, the delight of getting something you're excited to publish, the pride of holding a finished issue and knowing it wouldn't exist had you not put it together!

Allow me to quote from one of your typically flame-fanning editorials: 'I see the melting pot that is Oxbridge. I am looking at publishers' lists and seeing Oxbridge colleges [and] adopted performative identities.' I am empathetic. But how do you hope to stand against this, if it isn't by also considering poets' identities?

'Typically flame-fanning' – ha! I do like the editorial as a rhetorical pose to be struck with whatever degree of flair one can manage; I'd hate to be boring. In some ways identity is important to me; for instance, I want specifically to make space for Midlands writers, particularly early-career ones. The journal has always felt like something I'm doing for writers from where I'm from and who are like me in some ways – of an inner-city, working-class, immigrant background far removed from rarefied halls. There's some level of Brummie bloody-mindedness to it all. But my consciousness of identity and desire for the sort of people I see around my city to have a presence – rather than representation which is, I think, a false promise with unhelpful burdens attached – in the pages of journals is distinct from, say, regarding identity as some all-consuming, defining theme. The elaborate, obsessive, over-performed, narcissistic excess of popular identity discourse in its many guises bores me and its endless use to sell us everything from outrage to ideology to products is something I find cynical and approach with considerable scepticism. Yet it's another thing we all become implicated in. So, I consciously commission diversely and consciously commission writers who write well, have interesting things to say, and who I want to help develop. I hope others will then give opportunities to those writers.

When I reviewed your first year for the TLS, *I suggested that some of the better-known poets in your debut issue 'might have been approached in an attempt to give the issue ballast'. You later politely told me how wrong I was! How did those poets hear about the magazine?*

Yes, you mentioned Gregory Leadbetter and Alison Brackenbury. Greg is the lecturer I referred to earlier; he is Professor of Poetry at BCU, and the most brilliant scholar and poet I know. His seminar was the first place I ever shared a poem – he took my work seriously, which allowed me to do so. I've read horror stories about people's MFAs in the US, especially from writers of colour and women, but the MA with Greg was life-affirming and transformational. His belief in me is what gave me the confidence to do any of this. I fondly call him my Poetry Dad. So, the poem Greg sent was very much like your dad buying a drink from your lemonade stand to be encouraging. Alison saw our open submissions call on Twitter and, because she is tremendously generous, sent us poems and then travelled to Birmingham to read for our launch event, though we couldn't pay her travel let alone a reader's fee at that point. She's been very supportive and I'm grateful.

Which less well-known poets have you been particularly pleased to publish?

Many. I'm glad to have Vera Fibisan and Elizabeth O'Connor in issue six; Lucy Holme in issue seven. Recently I've been more focused on the prose in the journal. That's quite an undertaking and I think sets high-quality journals apart – there's far less room to hide in prose – and I've been pleased thus far. For many of the reviewers and prose writers we've published, their piece in *PBLJ* was their first in a literary journal: Adrian Earle, Khaled Hakim, Rupinder Kaur, Rochelle Roberts, Cuilin Sang, Sara Kazmi, Fahad Al-Amoudi, Reem Abbas, Barry Pierce, and Ibrahim Hirsi who is now Editorial Assistant at *PBLJ*.

'There's far less room to hide in prose'?

While it's true that the uninitiated might mistake highly conceptual work for something a five-year-old could do, it's equally true that some writers mask lack of ability behind hifalutin concepts, exposition on themes, or urgency of voice. There's no doing that with prose: any reader will know immediately that bad prose is bad. Subjectivity and taste doesn't come into it the same way, so there's no benefit of the doubt to be given when an essay is a mess. Though I've seen some shared and praised that prove me wrong...

How do you want Poetry Birmingham to address or augment our critical culture?

I'll resist making totalising comments; it's too easy to do and to counter. I think we tend to notice things that speak to our idiosyncrasies, what we enjoy or are particularly rankled by and, more than that, whatever has the strongest marketing and momentum behind it so is constantly thrust before us. That ubiquitousness acts to construct our ideas around what's significant – be it particular poets, books, themes or even features of the critical or wider culture. Whatever doesn't have that force in terms of marketing, presence, institutional support or popularity but ought to be noted as significant can escape our attention and the attention of editors and reviewers.

I felt I was reading reviews that were politely descriptive, obscured by academese, overstating praise, avoiding plain criticism: writing that was dull and lacked personality. I recently read the blurb for a workshop on reviewing and criticism which framed 'inadequate' reviews as those which are based more on opinion than evidence. I find that an odd way to think about poetry because what I expect from a writer *is* their subjective opinion; yes, with reference to the text that illuminates how they arrived at it but not an 'evidence-based' scientific argument that subordinates individual response to notions of objectivity. Criticism is about the critic as much as whatever they're writing about and that is okay, or even desirable, if the critic is interesting and enjoyable to read. I hope *Poetry Birmingham* can publish criticism that is enlivening, fun, illuminating, straightforward, gutsy, opinionated, clarifying.

I'm surprised you don't write more reviews. You're evidently not afraid to say what you think.

I review a little now. I've reviewed for the *TLS*, *PN Review*, *Modern Poetry in Translation* and *The Poetry Review*. I'm not afraid to say plainly that I've felt ill-equipped for it and it's been another accidental side occupation because editors have commissioned me. I don't have a degree in English Literature, haven't formally studied literary criticism, critical theory, etc; for many years I felt I wasn't qualified to write at all, let alone about other people's writing. My reading has chasms and the reading I have done and continue to do is lost so swiftly to my terrible memory that it distresses me. Reviewing requires slowing down, research – for everyone, I'm sure, but I feel its burden acutely. For what it's worth I can bring my honest readings and opinions to a review, though, provisional and partial as they may be.

Would those 'chasms' ever prevent you from taking on a commission to review a poetry book?

I've lost enough writing years to that. I take heart in looking to the autodidacts I admire and I'll take on any commission that interests me. If it involves things I don't feel confident about, I read and learn until I do. The best work one can do is that which expands one's knowledge and experience as a writer and person.

I've said no to things that I don't want to read even though they've won big prizes. If I have a strong sense that I'm not going to enjoy a book after reading extracts, I won't. Time is painfully finite and I don't wish to be shaped by fashions and peer pressure more than necessary.

Which poets do you return to most frequently?

I return to lots of (mostly dead) poets often but Frost, Hardy, and Tennyson are my holy trinity. I suppose I sought poetry with melancholy, music, darkness and doubt, so their work resonated and I felt an instant affinity. With Hardy, I first read *Tess* and knew there was no question I'd love the poems too – a matter of recognition and temperament, I suppose. I recognise there's an element of critical colour-blindness when it comes to the poets who are important to us. It may seem an odd thing to say but another thing I love about Tennyson and Frost is that they have poems children can understand, love and memorise, and I think that's valuable: poems to keep in the heart, and to share in the home.

In the editorial to issue 6, you write 'everyone is told to be your authentic self', but then you ask: 'what if one's self-preservation depends on not being too authentic or too much oneself – what if expressing oneself leads to vulnerability one isn't willing to risk or pay the price for?' What did you have in mind?

I was thinking about how we encounter the word 'authentic' in popular discourse and what feels like the false promise of externalising, labelling, and marketing our selfhood. False because it imagines the self as a static thing that can be declared and used as an aesthetic commodity and also because it imagines that process as something intrinsically moral and liberating. That perhaps works where the stakes are relatively low and there is greater social capital attached to whatever construction of identity one is leaning into. In some cases, though, the risks of saying what you believe or discussing aspects of who you are can be used against you, to devalue your work, or endanger your livelihood, liberty or safety. I think in any given political or cultural context writers have a clear sense of where the lines are and the costs of crossing them. Courage is more likely to lead to courthouses, poverty, ostracism and exile than stunning ad campaigns and lucrative deals, so I'm sceptical when politics is readily co-opted by corporate sponsors and when demands around politics are breezily placed on writers.

Your talk of social capital and marketing our selfhood makes me consider the effects on poetic discourse of social media. We have both been around long enough to remember an adult world without it. What influences do you think Twitter etc have on contemporary poetry and publishing, and why do you spend time on those platforms?

I didn't use Twitter before I needed some way into publishing and poetry. I knew 'Poetry Twitter' was how many people found opportunities so if I wanted writers and readers for *PBLJ*, I needed to be there. And it worked; Twitter is where we get many subscribers. However, there are things about it I definitely dislike; for instance, the culture of piling on. Mobs get very offended by being referred to as mobs, of course, but we've seen it happen often enough to recognise it as a behaviour pattern and acknowledge that it's easy for nuance to be lost and outrage to be currency on social media. People enjoy jumping into the fray when a target has been identified for uncharitable misinterpretation. You experienced some of that yourself and I've had it too and probably will again. Very early on I saw the entitlement some people felt in trying to chastise me for interacting with those, or in a way, they disapproved of, and how resistance to that results in being blackballed for failing to comply with the dictates of prevailing cliques and their dogmas. I care enough to be annoyed by malicious behaviour but not enough to kowtow to avoid being targeted; people are entitled to get mad and I'm perfectly happy for them to continue being mad but have become more unforgiving with the mute and block functions. But there are people I enjoy Twitter banter with, and it remains an important way to find writers and readers and share new writing.

You founded both the magazine and Pallina Press at the same time, with Suna Afshan. You now largely seem to have uncoupled: she runs the press and you the magazine. Why the change? Were two heads better than one at first?

There were four of us involved in some capacity at first: Suna, Adrian, Olivia, and I. We were all on the MA together, but it was Suna and I who were really invested in a hands-on way with editing and making, so it soon became just us. We founded the press in February 2020 in the hope of publishing pamphlets, and we knew that eventually we'd formally separate the two projects for practical reasons. Suna's interests lie more with the design of beautiful books and mine lie more with the critical aspects of a magazine. However, since then Suna fell ill with Covid and other projects she was working on took priority, so Pallina hasn't published any pamphlets yet. I'm sure it will soon. We're still very close friends above all else, and supporters of one another's work, but it also felt important to create professional distance because the extent to which people saw us as a couple and treated us as a couple rather than as two individuals did begin to annoy me. We are our own women. Our writing is very different. Our names don't always have to be mentioned in the same breath. In the same way that creative women are diminished by being framed as someone's wife, secretary or scribe, being seen primarily as part of a creative duo is not something I would allow.

Earlier, you said that for many years you didn't feel equipped to write at all. Your debut pamphlet-in-a-box was published in 2020. This includes the long 'Hered-

ity', the kind of retrospective poem a younger poet couldn't write. Do you think waiting to get going in print, however that might have occurred, had any benefits for you?

Are you calling me old, Rory? I won't have your readers thinking I'm any older than twenty-three. It wasn't that I waited to publish so much as my life and circumstances didn't allow it until recently. The benefit of coming to this as a second career is that I have life experience and perspective that gives me a sense of urgency, conviction, and obstinance in how I approach things. I'm not going to waste time with anything that isn't important to me and doesn't give me joy or satisfaction. I won't wait for anyone else to set the agenda, open doors or lead the way. I'm not going to write if I can't be honest and take risks and, right now, I'm willing to take those risks and lose (borrowing from Adele here).

Your new pamphlet, Litanies *(Guillemot, 2021), many of the poems in which develop from engagement with Islamic texts and songs, is startlingly uncompromising in places. In one poem, for example, you write 'Fiqh makes the munafiq' ('Islamic law makes the hypocrite', I gather, from your notes), and continue: 'I'm the hooded illusionist // and you a spectator watching me / fight against my own restraints.'*

I could talk more about these lines but I consciously want to resist appending any prose commentary to the poems in *Litanies*. The notes do enough to open up the language and references, I think, and the rest is always left to the reader.

Did you have any trepidations about publishing this pamphlet? You wrote somewhere that positive feedback from Muslim readers means a lot to you especially.

Trepidations would be putting it mildly. It's easy to be uncompromising within the privacy of one's notebook but bringing writing that emerges in a solitary and private space to publication is another matter entirely. I can't say I felt the religious culture and communities I've come up in nor the wider literary culture I participate in would be particularly receptive. But I hoped *Litanies* would find a sympathetic post-religious audience and remain invisible to easily offended dogmatists or zealots. Sometimes it can feel like a blessing that poetry has a niche audience.

The Circle and other poems

JANE DRAYCOTT

The Circle

In the circle one of the girls said
before this I was an accountant
and a vase
            and we knew
what she meant – something like
a multi-purpose function room
or how in a buffeting wind
                a tree is also
a ritual lion-dance performance.

The facilitator replied so let's
consider the relationship between a piece
    of pottery and the maternal womb

but the girl said no that's not it
more like isn't that amazing
        to be two things at once

like in the middle ages when bread
on the tongue was also the body
        and wine was the blood
and no fuss was made

because though you can count
the number of gates to the heavenly city
and be sure any storm will turn
        your small vessel to matchwood

of our fates we know actually nothing
and some seas might also be lakes
    with another encircling shore to set down on.

The Yard

Tethered as we were to the yard
of the city, something still lifted inside us
like weeds through concrete
till we were so filled up that fire caught

and we were aloft, the balloon-silk doming
over our heads as in our ears the spirits
of the guy-ropes cried out and split.

No sound then but the roar of the burner flames
as we rose past the counter-fall of offices
and treeless gardens, the houses under siege,

our childhoods emerging backwards
as we floated above the fireflies of the traffic
and the school grounds where on Fridays
the police had patrolled with their horses,

till at last the air froze around us, and all
we wanted was to lie again on the warm earth
in the parks, listening to the roots of the grass,

like returning sailors rounding the corner
to the last street before home,
thinking already about that other life at sea.

Wilderness

This message is like to be with you
later than I desire:
                    I have entered
a new wilderness – randomly generated
ravines, sunless abysses in the heart
of the financial sector, sirens throughout –
                    and am alone.

Yesterday I climbed the hill
above the house and went on
over the pass into the next valley,

a realm where not one person
has heard of our village, our rare Eden,
even though it is so close
                    as I have discovered.

I have asked the few strangers I meet
which way is the surest road back
to summer but nobody not one person
                    has the first idea.

O how I would like to be with you,
                    how I desire that now.

The Long Loft

*In natural science the principles of truth
ought to be confirmed by observation.
Carl Linnaeus,* Philosophia
Botanica *(1751)*

I'd gone up to see where the knocking
was coming from:
                    the long museum loft,
floating like a wide-bodied aircraft
above the kingdomed galleries below,

and from whose birds-eye windows
across the city's quartered A to Z I saw
that there were other kingdoms too:

the moving and the motionless, the speaking
and the silent, the living and the dead,
the kingdoms of the red and blue

and of the yellow with its scattered envoys
quietly everywhere – the trampled primrose,
brimstone in the early butterfly, the orpiment
in ancient glass –
                    first pigment to fade,
lifting off already, pale with February's trace.

I saw then what the knocking in my head might be
                    and from that date began to order, organise.

The Gleaners and other poems

ALISON FELL

Les glâneurs (The gleaners)

Snow came and went in the night
while we like beggars were
under our blankets, untouchable

Cold breath blows from the folded hills
on a village in quarantine, sealed doors,
streets quiet as field-stones

Between bare vine-rows, blue
sky-gates opening to the horizon

The tractor like a fishing boat
towing a wake of hungry gulls

The *terroir* tightening its belt,
the squirrel on its winter walnut trail

Mistletoe won't grow in salt air,
preferring the land-locked
banks of the Loire, its white berries
a banquet for blackbird and robin

So there you have it, in a nutshell –
everything reduced to what it can eat,
what it can glean from the garden,

what is toxic, and what is merely
a tempting memory of red apples,
those last bright lights of autumn

The Milkmaid

At the kitchen table she stays up late
by the rustle of the radio, counting dead
people – better to rely on your own rituals
than trust the government's

In the midnight interval between
the day before and the one to come,
where time stands still and lost things gather,

She sees her father on some long-ago Saturday,
his blunt stub of pencil ticking off the foot-
ball pools: Away-wins, draws, defeats

What were the odds when Jenner staked
his famous vaccine on the milk-maid's cow-
pox blisters, or when Fleming laid his bet
on penicillin moulds, grown painstakingly
in the pure tears of his co-workers?

This is the pattern of her life –
to consider the properties of ferments,
not to weep, but to calculate,

to measure raw milk from the jug,
make fresh yoghurt for the morning.

Agoraphobia I)

Snow feathering down on the *Autoroute,* thin, aimless,
falling without landing.

In the *Aire de Repos* an Arab boy lays out his prayer-mat,
anchoring it with his trainers against the wind.
His scowl says the snow doesn't belong to me, nor the forecourt,
nor the walkway leading to the concrete sanctum of the *Toilettes.*

Last night I dreamt that the *gîte* had no room for me.
When I spread my karrimat outside, they said the spot
was ecologically *protegé,* pointing to a pure white jay
nesting in a thicket of gorse.

The Arab boy, east-facing, bends and bends again to his
devotions. As I skirt his boundary my shadow – fainter
than snow, but flagrant – falls across his legs.

He doesn't need to flinch: already I'm seeing the word *Trespass*,
the forbidden thicket with its chastening thorns, his two bare
heels nesting there like eggs.

Agoraphobia II)

I lie with my cheek
to the pillow. I dream

of crossing the threshhold,
all naked and rosebud-nippled,

of standing at the door
to greet the rain.

Open Sesame!

My throat turns acrid, a war
of words taking my breath away.

My knees go A.W.O.L, my feet
wooden, rigid as idols.

Any step I take is a step too far.

Maybe the trick is to be
invisible, veiled even,

ooze under the barbed wire
like an oil-slick.

When I present my passport at the border,
no one has the authority to stamp it.

Who should I complain to?
In Kabul, the Taliban are

enjoying the Merry-Go-Round,
riding the little painted horses

After the War Is Over

ROBYN MARSACK

Kate Kennedy, *Dweller in Shadows: A Life of Ivor Gurney* (Princeton University Press, 2021)

The poetry of Ivor Gurney (1890–1937) is striking in its freshness and intimacy, in its conversational tone, its musicality; written out of deep shadows, seeking small contents and unchanging joys, it ranges from Severn to Somme, cabbages to Roman remains, as eclectic as its maker's mind. Here he is, remembering what it was like to carry all he thought requisite along with his soldier's gear:

(Yes, but when you have parcels, and there's half a
                                                                        cake

In your haversack, and Cobbett, Borrow and William
                                                                        Shake-
speare in your left pack, in your right Walt Whitman;
                                                                        [...]
A chess set hidden somewhere, and the Everyman
                                                                        Century
Of Essays stuffed in your tunic out of harm's way.

Who else sounds like this, of the First World War poets?
In 'The Bohemians', his sympathies lie with those who
'would not clean their buttons, / Nor polish buckles after

latest fashions' (whether deliberately or not, Gurney never quite reached required army standards himself):

> These were those ones who jested in the trench,
> While others argued of army ways, and wrenched
> What little soul they had still further from shape,
> And died off one by one, or became officers. [...]
> Surprised as ever to find the army capable
> Of sounding 'Lights out' to break a game of Bridge;
> As to fear candles would set a barn alight:
> In Artois or Picardy they lie – free of useless fashions.

The humanity, immediacy, individuality of the poem, in which Gurney's anger is transmuted into energy and elegy, shows him at his best – and indeed, this is one of three poems that recent anthologists have all chosen.

His stock – if we take First World War anthologies as a measure – is on the rise. By the time of Jon Silkin's influential and polemical *Penguin Book of First World War Poetry* (1979), he had half the number of Sassoon's poems; Isaac Rosenberg and Wilfred Owen were way ahead. Most recently, the Oxford World's Classic anthology edited by Tim Kendall features twenty poems by Owen, with Sassoon and Gurney both represented by seventeen (and Rosenberg down to nine). This slow rise was partly because Gurney's poems were difficult to find. The composer Michael Hurd's vivid, short biography, *The Ordeal of Ivor Gurney* (1978), could only point to a selection of mostly unpublished poems made by Edmund Blunden at the urging of the composer Gerald Finzi, issued in 1954, and about half of those plus a further ninety-seven previously uncollected poems chosen by Leonard Clark, issued in 1973. The manuscript collection deposited – after family ructions – in the Gloucester Public Library archives contains hundreds more. We had to wait another decade for a *Collected Poems*, chosen and edited by P.J. Kavanagh (1982, revised 2004). Kate Kennedy, who provides valuable chronological listings of his poetical and musical works in her new biography, maintains that Gurney's reputation, even now, 'is based on less than a third of his work, in both music and poetry'.

Kennedy argues that she is doing something new in presenting Gurney as 'an important cultural figure whose work helps us understand something about the intersections between mental illness, human relationships, landscape and war trauma'. Gurney, even in his sanest moments, had quite a high estimation of his own talents, but I hear him harrumph at 'cultural figure'. It seems to downplay the very particularity of his circumstances, which Kennedy then presents in great detail, and his achievements as composer and poet – a combination unmatched since the Elizabethans. Rather, she gives us perspectives on an incontrovertibly extraordinary artist, within a complicated set of human relationships: a countryman – like Edward Thomas and Edmund Blunden; an infantryman on the Western Front, the nature of whose trauma is not quite articulated in the book; and a man prey to mental illness throughout his life. She has divided her generally perceptive and richly informative (especially about the musical context) biography into three almost equal parts: soldier, civilian and asylum inmate, with a shorter section on Gurney's youth up to 1916.

He was rooted in his beloved Gloucestershire, yet Kennedy shows he never had a real 'home': not with his family, his quiet father (a tailor of Gloucester) overshadowed by his severe, distant mother; nor a settled place within the various families offering encouragement and warmth to which he attached himself as a young man. Gurney had supporters at the Royal College of Music: Sir Hubert Parry and Charles Villiers Stanford ('I love Gurney more and more. He's the greatest among you all, but the least teachable'), and later Ralph Vaughan Williams, a kindly and encouraging mentor as Kennedy shows, even in the asylum days. His attempt at living by himself in the country, in a miserable cottage, failed. He was discharged in October 1918 on a half-pension, on the grounds that his condition was 'exacerbated but not caused by' the war, and an aunt took him in, but that wasn't a success. He was awkward in ways that the highly socialised Owen, for example, was not. In and out of the RCM – London, its streets and company, always stimulated him but even in his student days overwhelmed him, so that he had to retreat to the country – and after the war in and out of work, as a farm labourer, a cinema organist, a tax clerk, Gurney could not hold on to his sanity. Like John Clare, he was locked away from the world, with few visitors during his fifteen years at the Dartford asylum.[1]

Donald Davie maintained that Gurney was not a war-poet or a nature-poet (Kavanagh nicely suggests that 'If he is to be given a locality, he could with more justice be called a sky-poet') but a post-war poet. Before the war, his efforts were all in the direction of music. The music, heroically, continued, despite three years in the army, nearly two of them continuously in the war zone. He managed to compose one song on active service, a setting of a poem by Masefield, 'By a Bierside' (August 1916). Hubert Parry found the song to be 'the most tragic thing he knew' when it was premiered at the RCM in Gurney's absence. As he headed towards the Somme in October 1916, he wrote to his friend and unwavering supporter Marion Scott, that when setting poems he must 'be able to live in the same atmosphere as that in which [the poet] wrote his poem, only – being musician, to have told my thoughts in another language'. The poem provided the necessary 'visions and vistas'. He admits, however, to being 'almost devoid of patience' with the process. 'The sad fact is that I do not know what it is to feel well, and what work I do has to be done in spasms very quickly over.' It wasn't just trench-life, it was Gurney's life condition, already evident at the RCM. As Kennedy makes clear, whatever his occasional arrogance and erratic behaviour, Gurney was recognised by contemporaries and elders as a remarkable musician.

He had always set poetry – by Henley, Stevenson, Bridges – and in the field of war he turned to writing it himself. His poems were first published in the Christmas edition of the RCM magazine in 1915. By 1917 he had a collection of forty-six poems accepted by Sidgwick and Jackson. Considering titles for this first volume, Gurney tried out 'Songs from Exile', Gloucestershire being constantly in his mind; 'Songs from the 2/5th', placing himself squarely amidst his fellow soldiers; and 'Strange Service' (under which title he submitted it), reflecting his unswerving devotion to England: 'who wrest my soul to serve you / In strange and fearful ways beyond your encircling waters; /None but you can know my heart [...] None, but you, repay.' Someone chose *Severn and Somme*, and there they were, the two poles of his experience.

In July 1917 he was describing his current location to Marion Scott as 'a country of faint continual haunting charm almost entirely of man's fashioning. A Scarlatti, early Mozartish atmosphere restful and full of home-sense, and heart-ache.' (Much of the liveliness of Hurd's biography comes from his liberal use of Gurney's letters, and I wished for more of them in Kennedy's.) The poetry is full of music, not only in its form but in its references; Bach and Beethoven were his lode-stars. Davie praises Gurney's striking first lines; Kavanagh his ability to close a poem brilliantly. If his early poetry was composed in the Georgian spirit, it also had unsettling reverberations that were to become more explicit. In 'Bach and the Sentry' for example, the second stanza seems simple enough: Gurney has been flooded with the recollection of a Bach prelude in the watches of the night:

> When I return, and to real music-making,
> And play that Prelude, how will it happen then?
> Shall I feel as I felt, a sentry hardly waking,
> With a dull sense of No Man's Land again?

We are left with a painful question: will the music, which came to him as delight in France, yet reminded him there of the distance he had travelled from any 'real music-making', remind him in post-war life only of that 'dull sense' of the night-watch and of the horrors he had seen? This is essentially trauma articulation: the impossibility of setting one thing in the past and one in the present, feeling the war experience as eternally and inexorably present.

Blunden, who noted the difficulties of Gurney's 'gnarled syntax', caught the complexity of Gurney's war service in his introductory memoir because it was so close to his own experience:

> [He] was with men of his own shire, in whom a like tradition and similar ability were personified, and we may see how the passage of his life as a soldier became a deep delight to him. When we observe that with it were mingled the extreme horror and futility of his battlefield days and nights, we apprehend the whole force of the period as it fastened upon his imagination [...]

Around 1925, Gurney writes in 'War Books' (which survives only in Blunden's transcription):

> Out of the heart's sickness the spirit wrote
> For delight, or to escape hunger, or of war's worst
>   anger,
> When the guns died to silence and men would
>   gather sense
> Somehow together, and find this was life indeed,

And praise another's nobleness [...]

He came to see himself as 'one of Five / War Poets' (in the tormented poem 'Armistice Day') and in all his wretched appeal letters from the asylum in autumn 1924, he claims to be 'The first war poet of England'. His poems relish the comradeship of men – not an eroticised experience; Kennedy conjectures he may have been homosexual by inclination but too ashamed to acknowledge it. Soldiers – Gurney remained a private – cooked together and sang together. In 'First Time In' he describes meeting the Welsh who gave them candles and rations and 'Sang us Welsh things [...] 'David of the White Rock', the 'Slumber Song' so soft, and that / Beautiful tune to which roguish words by Welsh pit boys / Are sung – but never more beautiful than there under the guns' noise.' And in 'Strange Hells' (the single Gurney poem in Larkin's *Oxford Book of Twentieth-Century English Verse*), he describes the Gloucesters going into their first engagement and managing to fire while singing 'That tin and stretched-wire tinkle, that blither of tune: / 'Après la guerre fini', till hell all had come down.' You can hear the irritated musician as well as the admiring comrade.

Like Blunden, Gurney in the post-war years could not help 'going over the ground again', but it was not his only subject. He wrote about Gloucestershire and the Cotswolds, London and – unexpectedly – America; described homely things ('The Kettle Song'; 'The different roof-sounds – house, shed, loft and scullery'; cabbages, tea, tobacco), reflected on music, musicians, and writers from Homer to Thoreau. His poetic gods eventually were Edward Thomas (whose widow gave such a memorable account of visiting him in Dartford, taking maps to trace the old routes of the indefatigable poet-walkers), Gerard Manley Hopkins, Walt Whitman and Ben Jonson.

The poems by Gurney that are common to several anthologies are 'To His Love', 'The Silent One' and 'The Bohemians'. The first was written when he was on a signalling course in England in 1918, and published in his second collection, *War's Embers* (1919). It begins as a conventional Georgian poem in rhyming quatrains:

> He's gone and all our plans
>   Are useless indeed.
> We'll walk no more on Cotswold
>   Where the sheep feed
> Quietly and take no heed.

There are three more quiet stanzas – 'But still he died / Nobly...' – and then the growing urgency of the final one, 'Cover him, cover him soon!' and the shock of the ending: 'Hide that red wet / Thing I must somehow forget.' I can never quite decide whether this ending – on an ignoble, dehumanised object, memorialised despite itself, as unforgettable as the boating days gone by – is stunning in its nakedness, or whether the rhyme, instead of clinching it, gives the poem a sort of bathos. Perhaps there is a touch of Sassoon's tactics, a powerful punch to floor the reader at the close.

The other two poems were written in a hugely productive asylum year, 1925. There are, wonderfully, in Gurney's poems glimpses of the uncowed self in circumstances framed to defeat him. 'The Silent One' – a man hanging silent on the wires who had once 'chattered through / Infinite lovely chatter of Bucks accent' (Gurney is always alert to the sounds men make) – shows him defiant; to the 'finicking' accent of one who requests him to crawl forward, he replies politely

'I'm afraid not, Sir.' There was no hole no way to be
                                                    seen
Nothing but chance of death, after tearing of
                                                  clothes.
Kept flat, and watched the darkness, hearing bullets
                                                whizzing –
And thought of music – and swore deep heart's deep
                                                    oaths
(Polite to God) and retreated and came on again,
Again retreated – and a second time faced the
                                                  screen.

Back to where he started, the dead man hanging on the wire, but in a complex human landscape of comradeship, class, survival instincts, trained musicianship; registering the likelihood of a torn uniform equally with the ex-cathedral-chorister's call upon God ('polite') and perhaps the very key of the bullets' sound.

Hurd, a composer himself, judged that Gurney's musical reputation rests on his songs, taking his place 'where, we must suppose, he would have wished' alongside such song-composers as Dowland, Parry, Finzi (who set some of Gurney's poems) and Britten, he finds the poetry much harder to characterise. Whereas he allows touches of 'genius' in the songs, he settles for Gurney's being a 'minor master' in poetry. Kennedy discusses his other work besides the songs – orchestral, chamber music, piano – with dutiful thoroughness, and makes higher claims for some of it. She relegates to a footnote Donald Davie's assessment of Gurney's work in 1925 as 'outdistancing' Eliot's and Pound's, making Owen's and Thomas's achievements 'appear slender' by comparison. Maybe not so minor, then! Davie's claims rest on a strenuous case for Gurney's craftsmanship, looking to the Elizabethans and Jacobeans as others did in the 1920s, but choosing the hard art of Ben Jonson in particular. Kennedy herself provides ample proof of his engagement with Shakespeare.

We can profitably look at Gurney's London poems with their allusions and references through a Modernist lens, as Davie insists, or indeed a poem such as Kennedy gives us, 'Iliad and Badminton' (from *Best Poems*, not in Kavanagh),[2] actually more about cricketers but speaking of legendary figures in sport and the arts (Kreisler, Whistler), and lost, lovely places in a seamless flow:

From dead Shrewsbury, as from the younger Grace
                                          memory winces –
But Gloucester, Cheltenham's way, with August stays
                                                  clearly;
Troilus walks white, Cressida truer watches him;
Agamemnon takes brute ease in the half crown
                                                  gallery –

Priam tells tales of Merton, Thornbury [...]

Kennedy's commentary on this poem makes the key point that the 'fearlessness' of the work written between 1922 and 1926 'might only have come from the removal of "normal" social, cultural and linguistic barriers.' She continues: 'In the grand tradition of Schumann and Beethoven, such mature, ambitious work can be better understood as "late" rather than "mad".' Despite some raggedness, Gurney was advancing his art in those asylum years – under the star of Whitman – and using forms that stretched to accommodate his asynchronous perspective.

We now have, in Kennedy's book, a definitive repository of knowledge about Gurney's life and works which deepens our understanding of both. If I was sometimes overwhelmed by the level of detail and her determination to give everyone their due, I was glad to find poems not included in other collections. It should be said that Princeton University Press has made it a handsome volume, well illustrated and indexed, and priced very reasonably. It is marvellous that Tim Kendall and Philip Lancaster are working on the *Complete Poetical Works* – so much depends, in Gurney's case, on the labour of editors – although at £120 (for the first volume, published by OUP in March 2020) it is a library/scholarly purchase. The curious reader must rely on Kavanagh's revised edition, and hope for an expanded one as the texts are established and brought to light. It is, after all, not useful to badge Gurney as 'war poet', 'nature poet', 'mad poet' and thus shelve him conveniently. Perhaps Hopkins has the best words for the work and the poet: 'All things counter, original, spare, strange; [...] swift, slow, sweet, sour; adazzle, dim [...] Praise him.'

1 The general assessment of Gurney's condition was the catch-all 'dementia praecox', before 'schizophrenia' or 'manic depression' became recognised diagnoses. The sketchy Dartford admission notes include: 'patient said to be a muscian'. Kennedy writes that there is no point in speculating on what might have happened if Gurney had gone to a different hospital in Edinburgh in 1917. Gurney was a private, registered as gassed and wounded rather than shell-shocked, and convalesced at the Bangour War Hospital, which accommodated 3,000 patients. It was no Craiglockhart, where Owen and Sassoon were being treated at the same time: that was for 'neurasthenic officers'.

2 This is a text from *Best Poems* and *The Book of Five Makings* (1995); the same editors, George Walter and R.K.R. Thornton reconstructed *80 Poems or So*, a collection that Gurney put together in 1922, but which was not accepted for publication then (MidNAG/Carcanet, 1992). Thornton also provided a scholarly edition of *Severn & Somme* and *War's Embers* (1987), following that with his edition of Gurney's *Collected Letters* (1991) – all MidNAG/Carcanet publications. (As were similar editions of John Clare, incidentally; a credit not only to various painstaking editors but to George Stephenson of MidNAG.)

King of Snake and other poems

ALEX MACDONALD

King of Snake

Yes I remember being hated
and life as the King of Snake
that internal rosebush feeling
looking in a mirror I saw scales
on my face each one a complaint
about someone I became again
I was used to transformation
other lives and circumstances
lover and gentle friend both
at times the under and over dog
up on the midnight mountain
I was reacquainted with these faces
feeling the kitchen sink emotions
and I wept before my slimy destiny
but it's thrilling being a Medusa Man
my forked tongue piercing words
every sentence covered in snake oil
each idea an umbrella opening indoors
I found out people loved to hate
it brought with it a harsh glamour
that made you scared to be alive
for fear of doing it all wrong
of course I got lonely laying eggs
in many well-meaning nests
I remembered my friends fondly
their faces lit by birthday candles
how I soothed their soft fretting
their domestic intimacies and tastes
how their endless nephews behaved
but by then I was coldblooded
a simpler life of sun then shade
the elbows and armpits of the day
were now meagre in their joys
my dreams were more complicated
featuring a cruelty with no horizon
I would wake up with a beehive voice
and a wild gravity chafing every step
I was ill at ease from all this shifting
and my heart was a wall-mounted bass
which sang 'don't worry be happy'
I don't remember my abdication
but how could I forget my old life
at my lowest tide it stayed anchored
eventually all the air was sucked up
from the shameful spaces of my heart
love became massive and unknowable
a forest of shipping containers filled
with people fighting their snakes
which has become very popular

The Light Abridged

I am beginning to embrace the mushroom spectrum.
My hot water bottle is named Cassandra and I breathe
like a cutlery drawer opening, closing. The neighbours
are italicised in the breeze. All my ideas have legs
and are walking away.

It's beautiful to care, beautiful to stop caring – to have a fat
spaghetti brain and witness the noodling. I have no choice
but to accept the evening's excess, its old wave.

See what you can make of the dream reruns, the familiar
venues where a grievance is unfolding. In the gathering,
I have made my choices. When did life become serious
origami, looking for an original crease, the hands
that made it so.

Voice Message

That summer you were everywhere like water,
swelling the walls and ruining park walkways.
I lay a puckered hand over these memories.
But it is good to feel elemental, to remember
a woman's blonde scarf waving hello on the beach,
where foam was collecting into temples. Not the
rooms with their prepared first impression, but
an idea of return. I am afraid I still have that
little determined complacency. I wandered into
a haunted house with a flooded basement and
accidentally stayed there for years. My attention
is dawdling outside the window. When will my
balloon regatta finally come?

Three Further Poems in English

MARK DOW

ASL

The sign for *Poland* – sorry to
say it – same as the sign for
breast. At least it's pretty close.

Auntie

Both. I speak both. I grew up in Hong Kong
So we speak Cantonese. But then in school
They taught us Mandarin so that's why I speak
Both. But honestly I think that Mandarin's
More beautiful. It's just more beautiful
The way it sounds. It goes like this. Just up
And down. It's smooth, you know? The Cantonese
Is harsh. Too sharp. It sounds too sharp. You hear
It, right? And Mandarin's the only language
That you use both sides your brain, both halves.
Most languages use one side. Because it's words
And also music too. That's why it sounds so
Beautiful. I think everybody agrees about that.

Broken

yeah
    I was born in Nigeria
and
    I came here when
    I was little
    I remember at the airport they asked us all these questions
and
    I just said whatever my mother said
    I just repeated what she said
but
    I didn't know what
    I was saying
    I couldn't speak any English
    I just spoke Broken English which is like English but no grammar no nothing
yeah
    Ibo State, Lagos
    It's a big city
yeah

Arnaut, *ara vos prec*

MICHAEL FREEMAN

Anno Dantesco celebrations ran apace, not least with Ned Denny's refashioning of the *Commedia* triptych into a sequence of blaze, bathe and bliss [*B After Dante*, Carcanet May 2021]. But now there's time to recall that singular moment in the *Purgatorio* when Dante doffs his cap to Arnaut Daniel. Arnaut: métier a troubadour-poet, manner the *trobar clus*, reputation *il miglior fabbro del parla materno* – the phrase which Guido Guinicelli coined about him, or rather which Dante coined for Guido to coin. I'll ask – *ara vos prec* – scholars to indulge a flâneur's unscholarly stroll round the block, folding Arnaut into layers of later writers, not least the bloc *[sic]* of totemic High Modernism. So then, just a ruminative homage for Arnaut, plainly unscholarly in not tabulating fairly obvious sources and side-stepping the hermeneutic thickets [*absit omen!*] of the *Commedia*'s allegorical schemata.

In the lockdown protocols of Dante's variant on Thomist eschatology, Arnaut is in purgatory on a charge of *luxuria*. Dante as the hard-travelling, hard-pressed participant-observer has just been lobbied by Guido Guinicelli, to whom he deferred as one ahead of the game in nurturing their *dolce stil nuevo*, to pause for a word with Arnaut. But then Dante as stage-manager goes so far as to frame Arnaut's intervention not in the *Commedia*'s Tuscan – the linguistic hegemony Dante was working to establish – but in Arnaut's own Occitan, or at least in Dante's pastiche of Arnaut's *langue d'oc*, albeit still in the *Commedia*'s terza rima, and taking the last line of the canto back into the narrator's Tuscan: *Poi s'ascose nel foco che gli affina*, as Arnaut is hidden again in purgatory's refining fire.

It's in canto xxvi of *Purgatorio*, the *regno secondo* where *l'humano spirito si purge*, that Arnaut is granted his moment, and after thanking Dante for that, he makes his plea:

> *Ieu sui Arnaut, que plor e vau cantan;*
> *consiros vei la passada folor,*
> *e vei jausen lo jorn, qu'esper, denan.*
> *Ara vos prec, per aquella valor*
> *que vos guida al som de l'escalina,*
> *sovegna vos a temps de ma dolor.*

[As Thomas Okey, Serena professor and basket-weaver, has it in my pocket 1901 Temple Classics: 'I am Arnault that weep and go a-singing; in thought I see my past madness, and I see with joy the day which I await before me. Now I pray you, by that Goodness which guideth you to the summit of the stairway, be mindful in due time of my pain.']

Dante wants to name and fame Arnaut – *al suo nome il mio desire/apparecchhiava grazioso loco* – though Longfellow, in the notes to his version of the *Commedia*, thought the only reason for letting Arnaut speak here in his own language was that Dante simply liked the sounds of the Occitan and the 'peculiar flavour' they give to the close of the canto. But Dante had already acknowledged Arnaut several times in his *De Vulgari Eloquio* – which Basil Bunting reckoned made later literary criticism redundant – while establishing the case for an 'illustrious vernacular' to stabilise an Italian language for literary and more prosaic purposes, in effect the dominance of the Tuscan over the regional vernaculars: a pitch for a cultural hegemony as Gramsci saw it, or purifying the dialect of the tribe, *pace* Eliot and Mallarmé.

The moment is a palimpsest: Dante the author becoming Dante the character becoming Dante the narrator in his grand theologico-anthropology of the good, bad and the sinfully ugly. He turns the plot so that the one purgatory-serving poet, Guinicelli, will prompt the encounter between two others in a *cosa nostra* of professional esteem. Much of the *Commedia* is settling old scores, but here it's giving credit where it's due. As to why Dante, and indeed Petrarch too, had thought so very highly of Arnaut, Longfellow, this time as professor of Italian, cites Raynouard, the pioneer of Romance linguistics: 'In reading the works of this Troubadour, it is difficult to conceive the cause of the great celebrity he enjoyed during his life.' Certainly Arnaut's *trobar clus* with its flamboyant technical adroitness, lexical exuberance and some opacity contrast sharply with the qualities of disciplined precision and lucidity that Eliot went on to find in Dante; and Virgil, Dante's 'Leader' through purgatory, might have found Arnaut hard to stomach. But Ezra Pound, staking his own 1913 claims as quality-surveyor of troubadour territory, thought Arnaut 'the best artist among the Provençals, trying the speech in new fashions'. Guinicelli slightly qualifies his praise of Arnaut as *il miglior fabbro de parla materno* in specifically *versi d'amore e prose di romanza*, though that's precisely in the popular sub-genres that his audience was paying him for. Arnaut takes the convention, makes a living from it, but pushes it on, a case of tradition and the individual talent if not quite what Eliot meant.

The handing down of the *il miglior fabbro* soubriquet through Dante from Guinicelli to Arnaut and then to Pound by Eliot is an intriguing tradition. Harold Bloom's pontifical taxonomy of devices by which 'strong' poets seek to cope with 'the anxiety of influence' had offered *apophrades*, confronting the discomforting weight of their legacy by taking on a deliberative conversation with their precursors to establish their own distinctive stance. We might wonder whether this ensemble of poets, if they had felt such 'anxiety' a*vant la lettre* of Bloomian theory, betray a trace of such *apophrades* with Arnaut as their ur-text, but it's simply that reading them now throws up an intertextual collage of deference, allusion, echo. Eliot took *Ara vos prec* as the title for his 1920 short collection; *The Waste Land* incorporates *Poi s'scose nel foco che gli affina,* and it's the line behind *Little Gidding's* redemption through fire; then a further allusion to the *Purgatory* besides three more to the *Inferno* are all flagged up in *The Waste Land* notes. In his 1929 essay on Dante, Eliot highlights the Arnaut moment as 'superb verses' and one of 'the high episodes'. Writing of what Pound called his 'revivication' of Provençal poetry, Eliot admits that he himself knows nothing of the language except for a few lines in Dante, but presumably this episode provided some of those lines.

Besides the insertion of Arnaut's own language, there's a glimpse of the man to be teased out of the encounter. His *ara vos prec* isn't a plea for some fast-track out of purgatory; after all – though the all wasn't over yet – he's in the seventh, the uppermost level of Purgatory, working out his repentance in hope – *e vei jausen lo jorn, qu'esper, denan* – not suffering the unfairness Empson noted: 'This last pain for the damned the Fathers found: /They knew the bliss with which they were not crowned.' And he reminds Dante, and Guinicelli if he might still be listening in these echo-chambers, of his professional reputation in the troubadours' tradition – *que plor e vau cantan* – though his earlier weeping and singing were in secular stories, and now facing a longer weeping for his spiritual needs. He's given just a walk-on part now, but it's still a moment to be able to affirm what he's done for his trade and his language. [Again, the temptation is to speak of him here as though he's a character, not a card in the pack that Dante's teleology deals.]

'Superb verses' or not, this moment of Arnaut's dialect has caused something of a problem for translators, which a few instances make clear. John Ciardi in his 1961 version argues that this language would strike Dante as courtly but rather antique, so Ciardi tries what he describes as 'a desperate attempt at bastard Spenserian' offering 'And by that eke virtue, I thee implour, / that redeth thee, that thou amount the staire, / be mindful in thy time of my dolour.' Geoffrey Bickersteth in his 1955 version of the passage offers what he describes as a Chaucerian stylisation: 'Now, preie you, by that power whiche not in vayn/up this high montaigne-staire hath lad you sure,/bethynke you in due sesoun of my payne!' And Cary's 1910 version more soberly proposes 'I pray ye by the worth that guides you up/Unto the summit of the scale, in time/Remember ye my sufferings.' Longfellow had his professorial reputation to guard so in his 1867 version had been even more cautious, preferring to leave the passage in the main text in the Occitan, relegating his own translation to a mere footnote: 'Therefore do I implore you, by that power/which guides you to the summit of the stairs/Be mindful to assuage my suffering!' with scarcely any attempt to catch some antique strangeness. Clive James's symbiosis of translation and exposition provides 'That you will think of, and have understood/ In time, my sins and penitential cares.'

That was the matter of handling Dante's pastiche of Arnaut's intervention in the narrative. When it comes to translating Arnaut's actual poems, Pound is the striking instance. His versions offer to embody the poet as jongleur and juggler, not at all uncomfortable about the translator's usual dilemma of striking a balance between the literal and the 'materiality' of the original. Where

Arnaut is occasionally arcane, a characteristic of the *trobar clus,* Pound's versions often make it more arcane still. It's often enough hard to know where Arnaut leaves off and Pond takes off on his own orbit, his accretive amplitude. Arnaut proposes, Pound disposes. But he's insistently setting out to catch the sound-stitching and muscular syntax, the articulate energy [*pace* Davie], and if that entails dislocating then re-assembling a text, so be it. The opening lines of *Doutz brais e critz* he renders as:

'Sweet cries and cracks
And lays and chants inflected
By auzels who, in their Latin belikes,
Chirm each to each, even as you and I
Pipe toward those girls on whom our thoughts attract;
Are but more cause than I, whose overweening
Search is toward the Noblest, set in cluster
Lines where no word pulls awry, no rhyme breaks gauges.

No cul de sacs
            Nor false ways me deflected
When first I pierced her fort within its dykes...'

where the lays and chants become the chirm/songs of the auzels/ousels/blackbirds, and can lead to piercing a fort and dykes – the poem as a seduction strategy.

Or again, Pound turns the close of '*Sim fos Amors*' as

Pouch-mouthed blubberers, culrouns and aborted,
May flame bits in your gullets, sore yes and rank
T'the lot of you, you've got my horse, my last
Shilling, too; and you'd see love dried and salted.
God blast you all that you can't call a halt!
God's itch to you, chit-cracks...'

Raimon de Durfort, with whom Arnaut had been a player in a celebrity debate-poem of his time, records that before becoming a travelling songster, Arnaut had been a promising student ruined by the dice and playing shut-the-box, perhaps one strand of that *passade folor* he confessed to Dante. Gossip about his personal life in the courtly ambience of twelfth century Provençe was no doubt enhanced by his poems where cheerful hedonism plays out in erotic imagery: ladies' chambers are to be penetrated by rods and nails. But the sketches on contemporary manuscripts are quieter images of a slight and willowy figure, gesturing as though performing his lyrics or with the set patterns of rhetorical gesture laid down in the handbooks. He's portrayed like a minor figure in a Sienese predella of the period, dressed in long tunic and surcoat, a loose chaperon topping his coif, though probably such representations are from stock illustrations in the dress and posture of troubadour stereotypes, the brand image. In contrast, there's one image of a more robust, impressively dressed figure, maybe well-attired to promote his current patron, self-possessed and ready for any *luxuria* on offer. One haggard close-up portrait seems to capture his pain in purgatory, but this turns out to be a modern painting of a modern namesake; purgatory isn't unknown even now.

Less speculatively than the portraits, Arnaut is held to have invented the sestina, though he might have been intrigued by Empson's throw-away remark after a luminous account of Sidney's double-sestina: 'the capacity even to conceive so large a form as a unit of sustained feeling, is one that has been lost since that age.' This sounds rather like the quasi-historicism of Eliot's 'dissociation of sensibility', but in any event it didn't close the door. Pound trawling round early Italian verse wrote his 'Altaforte' sestina, though he was a late-comer in the field: Spenser had incorporated the sestina in his 'Shepherd's Calendar' and Sidney had constructed the double sestina for his dialogue between Strephon and Klaius. Rossetti, prolific translator of early Italian poets and whom Pound considered the 'mother and father' of his own grasp of Tuscan poetry, translated Dante's own sestina. Swinburne of course made the most of any such form that allowed a rolling secular ritual, and even Kipling tried his unlikely hand, with a tramp's demotic almost claiming that the world is best seen as a book [Mallarmé again?]. The sestina's insistence on playing on the repeated words is an instance, rather like the villanelle, of incrementally teasing out their meanings, so they're not merely repetitions, allowing Empson to have his characteristic fun in teasing out a handful of connotations for each of the twelve recurring words in Sidney's double sestina. The sestina is, then, a form of *luxuria* in its technical seductiveness [a poetic sublimation of Arnaut's inclinations?], its constrictions demanding in the interlockings of repeated lines and rhyme-schemes but also allowing enough variability to extend the reach its protocols offer with a logic that keeps coming round on you. The form, attractive in its bravura, even exhibitionism, is just what a poet-troubadour-performer could make the most of. With Arnaut *il primo fabbro,* the sestina is still having a good run for its money.

Auden and Ashbery wrote their sestinas early on in their careers, perhaps muscle-flexing, but good examples of the notion [Empson's again] that good poetry is usually written from a background of conflict. Auden's 'Paysage Moralisé' and Ashbery's 'The Painter' both deploy topographies as tropes for the unresolved conflicts that their sestinas tease out and turn over, Auden's with the gnomic hieratic stance of his mid-1930s style, ending 'And we rebuild our cities, not dream of islands', Ashbery building his narrative of the artist's quarrel with his art until 'the sea devoured the canvas and the brush / As though his subject had decided to remain a prayer'. Elizabeth Bishop's sestina reaches an envoi Arnaut would have recognised: '*Time to plant tears* says the almanac.' Hecht uses the form as variously as a relaxed account of a cityscape in 'Sestina d'Inverno' but also in his 'The Book of Yolek' of a Holocaust victim. Kinsella's sestina about a death by snakebite closes with something of a Dantesque grimness: 'a sadness unwilling to release: the young soul's penetration / of *mala prohibita*'s venom. The lightness [*mala in se*] bites.' And this is only in the Anglophone tradition.

In the envoi to his '*Sim Fos Amors*' he somewhat ruefully admits:

Arnautz a faitz e fara oncs atens,
Qu'atenden fair pros hom rica conquesta
[Arnaut has waited and will carry on waiting /
Since it's through waiting that a wise man gets a grand victory']

which Pound – stretching for the rhyme – turns as:

Arnaut has born delay and long defence
And will wait long to see his hopes well nested.

Well, that charge in purgatory was for being lasciviously too well nested, and his poems were a well-woven nest from which, as *Briggflatts* has it, 'the spuggies have fledged'. Dante wasn't the first to praise him, but arranging for Arnaut's shade his norm-breaking moment in the *Commedia* was to accord him *l'omaggio ultimo.*

Dead Deer and other poems

JAMES WOMACK

Cold

It was a smug film, smug on its own evil, fat with it,
the actor-king so smug, the direction, allegedly so cold, so pure,
in fact only smug-drunk on its ambience of slush and nicotine,
springtime and grey city light and all the poor beige suicides,
the camera always moving, side to side, more fear, more broken
people, the surrounders, who indulged their man's brokenness,
the always sense of a wink to the camera, of men complicit in their
acting, their actions. *I want to know nothing* – this is not grief,
this is a teenage boy's, an Italian's fantasy of grief, how to weaponise
grief, grief as the royal road to a woman's body – and we tell the
audience that she is unsatisfied, and she keeps coming back
doesn't she, she's asking for everything that is filmed and shown,
and the great statue, Brando collapsing, Brando shouting,
the reason for all this, the centrepiece, his grunting
the audible sign of a *great actor*, just how close can you approach
a full contempt for the audience and still pivot on their love,
Brando grunting and dangerous even through the screen. One moment
in this vast smug film, black stain on the negative, when
I tell you I felt as pure a cold as any art has ever made me feel,
when Jeanne shouts across the metro station, a train passing,
to her useless and aggressive boyfriend, screams in a fury she
deserves *je suis fatigué de me faire violer* | *I am tired of being raped*
and the train passes and she has her fury out in the world
and that clever-clever camera switches to show how she is seeing
and there is no one standing or listening on the other platform.

And I saw this film in the cold cinema, the Spartak cinema,
the unheated former Lutheran church on Kirochnaya Street,
in 2001, before it was destroyed in an insurance fire,
in spring, almost spring, I was unhappy, not that unhappy, in love.
The film a scratched print, the sound horrid, the underpaid
abused *lektor* read out the script in a dry Russian monotone,
and the film was so cold, the church so cold, the camera eye so too...
I did not deserve to feel so cold, but what saved me was the world
existing outside the film, the cinema, the church, the abyss,
that voyeur, always ready with a few home truths, and to know that
yes, there was always standing and listening and watching,
and you can see the world without judgement and knowledge, it is not
all grey and tired, even in the grey-tired, grey-skinned city.
I came out into the grey evening, and forced myself to see life,
and that evening the bridges opened like a great stone bible,
and the river, the frozen river, the river, tore pages from itself.

Dead Deer

Great stuffed wineskin of a deer, dead deer, lying up against the fall,
next the lost punt pole and the abandoned tyre, tyre bleached in the sun,
water running over the weir, over arched-back head and body, the body swollen
little more each day, the eyes and bent legs oddly untouched, the deer still,
perfect, still perfect. I pray to this idol, little god of defeat, father of our failures,
overseer of the torn and defeated, shattered vase, vestigial tail;
I stand there daily to look at it, the whittering of pigeons under the bridge,
the same pigeons, children, great-grandchildren of the birds there
when I threw an engagement ring off the bridge eighteen years ago,
pigeons who exploded in an applause of wings and sour sheet metal
against the grainy sky of the five a.m. sleepless walk, walk whose only purpose
was the deliberate loss of the ring, and now, useless, I am married to her:
find someone you like to look at who doesn't hate you, they said. Enough.
The deer has been there four or five days now, hardly Shakespeare,
hardly enough to build a religion on; heron ignores it, mallards skim by.
I walked out this morning, to go to town, to pass the weir, to see the silenced
muntjac, vast as a dog, unnatural, bloated, silent, placid, unlikely seed:
the cat stood at the top of the stairs, and as I left I stroked him
and *love* he said *you think I need your love?* The cat stood at the top of the stairs
as I passed by, sardonic, alone, unopened, unfair, turning his head against me,
when other times, other days, he presses his mouth into my palm,
silences himself, growls within himself, sits on my lap when I try to teach.
Blockade cat, blunt cat against my walking. The river says you are married.
I dreamt for a while that a gigantic fish would swallow the ring, that I would live
to see somewhere in the *faits divers*, the local news, the miraculous story,
the gutted fish and a triumphant Polish fisherman, silent and sardonic
holding the carat and a half between two slabby fingers. It never happened;
my son still dreams of dredging the river, as if time did nothing and the river
flowed too slowly to lose the ring again. The river says again that you are married.
You can argue all you want; house and wife, libraries, shared children,
you are married, the pillow is never alone again, the dead breast is yours alone.
Stuffed, swollen wineskin of a deer, muntjac, dead, pushing up against the weir:
God's kingdom advances through glorious victories, cleverly disguised as disasters.

When Adam delved and Eve span,
who would gild the marzipan?

Summer Nights

1.

I swallow a pill filled with black television static. In my situation notebook, before the scholarly exercise breaks down into vague sketched parallel lines, there is a comment: 'Marvellous nightmares!' The handwriting is not mine.

My daughter eats cherries like something out of *La Bohème*. Another speckled handkerchief drops to the floor. She gives a vast, contented, operatic sigh, then reaches her determined fat-knuckled hand to the bowl again.

At the beginning of all this, I went for illicit dawn bike rides down empty B-roads. I crossed the motorway bridge with no traffic underneath me; stopped once dead at a vast buck hare, calm in the middle of the tarmac.

Of course, an anagram of the whole Bible would also be the whole Bible.

I have recently discovered Berlioz's *Les nuits d'été*. As with all new art, I wait for someone to tell me that my taste is faulty; that I cannot, must not, am simply forbidden from enjoying them.

I want to say something here about my father.

2.

I have to learn new techniques to think about my family. I cannot, must not live always along the same metaled ways. I must stop e.g. thinking of my parents as boring, start thinking of them as cruel.

I find my daughter with a recognizable face – my own face, when I am caught in some avoidable naughtiness. With my little finger I remove a cheerfully disarticulated woodlouse from her mouth. The thorax bitten into three crunchy chunks.

I cannot rely on my own powers of criticism. Not here, not in 'real' life. What I need is extra: a loose word or an unguarded comment will do, in default of a full deathbed confession.

The old riddle talks about cherries. You begin with a handful of flesh, and end with a few scattered jack-bones.

Evenings when we didn't play backgammon, we would play Scrabble. I would always lose. The draughty table, the concentrated silence. The avant-jazz of a butterfly trapped in the paper lampshade above us.

Or else this: the broad empty road underneath me; too early for birdsong. Two sinister motionless herons. A light moving in the sky.

3.

Nothing ever as empty as those darktime streets. Even the golden light in the window, the *sotto voce* hum of some recorded opera... even this is not enough. You start to believe in the patchy folk history of this area: weird beasts in the fields, the one-eyed dog.

For some people, his knowledge and sympathy is immense. Others are accepted on sufferance, if at all. I know that the open scars in my knowledge are things he has agreed to ignore; the mask slips occasionally. You should suffer fools joyously.

We're not getting out of this alive. Fortune favours the grave. #NoLivesMatter

I cannot remember if I was given a knife. Probably not: we pulled apart terrified buds of the hollyhocks with our nimble childish fingers. The colour was never inside them, never the deep cherry-stain we desired. Hollyhocks and honesty both.

We ordered the detritus in such a way as to tell the future. Poor man, beggarman.

Auguries are always unreliable, as unreliable as good taste. The sibyl, with god-aid, speaks with her maddened lips things both blunt and serious. The *tausenjähriges* reach of her voice.

4.

For *x* read *y*. Story of my life.

Before all this began, in heat, I walked five miles to the isolated boarding-house. Luck had me meet her on the road, slightly tipsy, freewheeling. 'What, are *you* here!' I have often played that curt sentence in my head, reading and misreading its emphasis.

The morning greets us with a glass of water and a bowl of fridge-cold cherries. Desultory love-talk before the inevitable, clandestine parting.

So many things I have kept from those closest to me, among which a reassessment of who those closest to me really are. Close in terms of affection, or close in terms of likeness?

After one such disaster, a trip to the chemist for Duprisal 30. The motherly pharmacist, a man approaching retirement, takes her by the sleeve and says 'Now, don't do that again, eh?' I had not thought her so obedient.

Another curtailed fatherhood. Duprisal, reprisal ... Something along those lines.

5.

Oh, headlong immorality! Oh, driving license!

I gave my truncated Oberon, in a production that I insisted no one come to see. I remember very little. 'Of thy misprision must perforce ensue | Some true love turned, and not a false turned true.'

In the sweated bedroom, the shared flat, there was always a video on in the background. For some weeks it has been *Without a Clue*, or else *Magnolia*, or else *The Matrix*. Writing this, it has taken me some time to remember these titles. Rabbit holes, rabbit holes.

From the roadside. Hare forms in the grass. A slight depression. *Nadie nos ha visto.*

Brother of mine lives now in a village, just too far to reach easily by bike. I am in awe of how he has gathered a family to himself, working with children and animals.

A themed picnic for his daughter's first birthday. Salami, lollipops, cherry pie, sausages, all with neat holes eaten through them.

6.

At the beginning of all this, I was alone and dazed. On the evening after the vote, I ate a bowl of ripe, solid cherries macerated in dark rum and dark sugar. A little expensive vanilla ice-cream. *My* world was alright, for a few minutes.

He flies like Icarus. Alas for his wings!

Slower now than he was, and less present. How much of a person's existence depends on others' noticing them? Old men ought to be spies.

But maybe I have been wrong the whole time? I remember when I was a child, enthralled, waiting for the next gnomic clue, scrap of wisdom. A few words in that calm, slow voice. I built a world on them, a religion. And now, hardy recusant, loyal dunce, I worry the façade is all there is, all there ever was.

I saw him from behind, riding his bicycle up the only hill. I could have overtaken him walking. You cannot see my face.

Neat in a box, with many lids like little television screens. Medicine to walk you from Monday to Sunday.

7.

A handful of pills; a handful of cherries; a handful of pills. Anita eats cherries like Mimi. My son told me a joke, his version of a joke: *Who was the first man to die? God, because he had to die to become God*. I felt nothing except knowledge and terror.

The lights failed halfway round his circuit, and he rode the last seven miles in frightened darkness, hoping for the dawn at every corner. Calmed himself, partially, by remembering crossword clues.

A book on 'the soul of rugby', *Muddied Oafs*. I misread the title as *Murdered Osiris*. Now, *there's* something to tell the old man!

Reviews

Quite Haunted

Frederick Seidel, *New Selected Poems* (Faber) £18.99
Reviewed by Ian Pople

Frederick Seidel's *New Selected Poems* reproduces poems
from his first volume *Sunrise* published in 1980, through
to his last volume *Peaches Goes it Alone*, published in
2018. That's some 260-odd pages for a career that's last-
ed forty years, with fifteen individual collections and
two other *Selected*s. Inevitably, perhaps, the first volumes
of such a fluent career are more pared than the later
ones. Even from the beginning, there is in Seidel's work
an enviable combination of observation and imagina-
tion. That combination in the early writing throws up a
kind of Dali-esque surrealism, in which there is striking
visual detail, with a grasping for juxtaposition.

Seidel's first book, *Sunrise,* contains the long title
poem, which begins, 'The gold watch that retired free
will was constant dawn, / Constant sunrise. But then it
was dawn. Christ rose, / White-faced gold bulging the
horizon / Like too much honey in a spoon, an instant /
Stretching forever that would not spill', and actually the
sentence does not end there. Such writing seems to seek
interpretation; that the 'gold watch' is a symbol of retire-
ment from work that offered the free will that was
'retired' with the watch's acquisition. Then, there is a
turnaround conjunction 'but' which, coupled with
'then', suggests a different kind of 'dawn', i.e. one that
rises with the coming of Christ. That coming, in turn,
seems to offer eternity. And there is a lot more of this,
in ways which seem to nod towards autobiography locat-
ed both around the world and in various times, the
details piled one against another. And, suitably perhaps,

the poem ends with 'I wake beneath my hypnopompic
erection, / Forty stanzas, forty Easters of life, / And smile,
eyes full of tears, shaking with rage.'

Perhaps 'Sunrise' was an early exercise in catharsis.
However, autobiography is never far from the surface of
Seidel's poems. And it is, perhaps, the confessional that
tinges so much of Seidel's poetry. It would be too easy
to ascribe this to Seidel's sense of Robert Lowell as a
model. But Lowell's presence can be felt throughout this
volume even down to word choice. Seidel's poetry is,
therefore, controversial because he is never afraid to put
the accoutrements of his clearly privileged life into his
poems. These are not simply the Ducati motorbikes that
he writes about with such affection. Seidel has led a life
amidst the Ivy League East Coast elite and it is his obser-
vations about those people and those things that, on the
surface at least, constitute his subject matter. It is true
that Seidel is never afraid to ironize both the subjects of
the poems and his attitudes to them. But if you read
Seidel, these are the things that, almost exclusively, he
has written about since those first books.

Clearly, confession does not necessarily make good
poetry. And Seidel's confessional aesthetic is very differ-
ent from, say, Frank Bidart. Seidel has little of Bidart's
raw, interiorised edge. Seidel's world and perhaps the
success of his writing is exteriorised. And that exterior
world is an excitement for Seidel, an excitement that he
has used throughout his collections. 'At Gracie Man-
sions' from his fourth collection, *Going Fast*, begins, 'I
like motorcycles, the city, the telephone. / TV but not to
watch, just to turn it on. / The women and their legs, the
movies and the streets. / At dawn when it's so hot the
sky is almost red. / The smell of both the rivers is the
underworld exhumed.' The observation moves from the
generalisation of the first line to the more particularised
detail of the women and their legs.' It then jinks side-
ways to 'the movies and the streets'. This opening stan-
za then ends with that almost thunderous final line
about the smell of the rivers, the 'both' locating it in New
York. Seidel is, perhaps, able to make the poetry con-
vince almost because of this excited moving from object
to object, from the general to the particular. And imbued
in all this is the chancy eroticism of both the women's
legs and that smell of the underworld.

This technical ability runs through much of the poetry in this book, making it substantial in many ways. There is a sense that Seidel is actually quite haunted by much that happens to and around him, and that he is almost a medium who explores that haunted and fiercely contemporary world.

Sunglasses

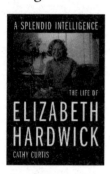

Cathy Curtis, *A Splendid Intelligence: The Life of Elizabeth Hardwick* (Norton) £25.00
Reviewed by Tony Roberts

As a writer, Elizabeth Hardwick (1916–2007) showed an impressive critical intelligence, her work stylish, experimental – and tough. She was married to Robert Lowell from 1949 to 1972, a recurrently traumatic experience given his bipolar episodes, which she handled with courage and dignity. Their marriage also promoted her career and influenced its thematic concerns.

After a Kentucky childhood and time spent at the universities of Kentucky and Columbia, Hardwick dropped her studies to concentrate on a writing career in fiction and criticism. Eventually she found her way into the circle of the anti-Stalinist left *Partisan Review*, and went on to co-found *The New York Review of Books* in 1963. Her pieces on literary, social and cultural subjects have most recently re-appeared in *The Collected Essays* (2017). There were also short stories, three novels (the last, the admired *Sleepless Nights*) and a biography of Herman Melville.

The essays are Hardwick's most enduring work. When in admiration – on Margaret Fuller, Simone Weil, Billie Holiday, for instance – she wrote with memorable subtlety. Of William James, whose letters she edited, she offered: 'An equable, successful man is not the ideal subject for portraiture, perhaps, but in the case of William James there is something more: a certain unwillingness to take form, a nature remaining open to suggestion and revision.'

Alternatively, Hardwick could be ruthless: on the 'sluggishness' of book sections, on theatre and contemporary authors (including fellow Southerners, Faulkner and Capote). Even her close friend Mary McCarthy suffered a merciless parody. Later, making amends, she could not resist a gentle barb on how McCarthy loved to take fictional revenge on her ex-husband, Edmund Wilson: 'She has disguised him in satirical portraits in her fiction, a disguise on the order of sunglasses.'

When they met in January 1949, Robert Lowell described her as 'slip-shod, good humored, malicious (harmless) and humorous – full of high-spirits'. In 'Man and Wife', he would recall that vivacity:

> ... Oh my *Petite*,
> clearest of all God's creatures, still all air and nerve:
> you were in your twenties, and I,
> once hand on glass
> and heart in mouth,
> outdrank the Rahvs in the heat
> of Greenwich Village, fainting at your feet –
> too boiled and shy
> and poker-faced to make a pass,
> while the shrill verve
> of your invective scorched the traditional South.

With Lowell's friends – Randall Jarrell, W.D. Snodgrass and Frank Bidart among them – Hardwick was not always popular. She appears to be the nurse-wife in Jarrell's 'A Well-to-Do Invalid', likened to 'a plaster Joan of Arc'. To some critics her marriage to Lowell, like her early affairs with Philip Rahv and Allen Tate, had a calculating edge. In truth, Hardwick's view of Lowell was never short of loving admiration, even after enduring the humiliation of Lowell's *The Dolphin* (1973), with its misuse of her letters. As Mark Krupnick suggested in a *Guardian* obituary, Hardwick made 'personal loyalty her own highest value'.

In Cathy Curtis's admiring *A Splendid Intelligence*, Lowell is present in two hundred of its three hundred pages, since Hardwick's reputation is based largely on work written during their years together. Without him, there seems a loneliness in her. (Is it idle to note that in the thirteen photos reproduced for the book, she is alone in nine and with Lowell in two of the others? Or that their daughter, Harriet, makes numerous but very brief and silent appearances?)

Curtis takes Hardwick out of her victimhood, to show us the talented and successful writer she was. She does this with some care, but tends to be too defensive at times of Hardwick's behaviour and of her feminist credentials. Like her friends Hannah Arendt, McCarthy and Susan Sontag, Hardwick remained suspicious of second wave feminism, taking an individualistic line.

More interesting are Curtis's pages on the impact of Hardwick at Barnard. Charismatic and demanding, she was certainly respected by many of her talented students. One, the writer Elizabeth Benedict, described her 'languid Kentucky drawl, her easy laughter, and her unvarnished criticism, delivered with a disarming originality that took away some of the sting'. This biography would have benefited from more eyewitness testimony.

Inevitably there is an imbalance in the weight of scholarship on Hardwick and Lowell. *A Splendid Intelligence* lacks the immediacy of the already published – and more substantial – Lowell biographies, and certainly that of all the letters available: Hardwick and Lowell's (*The Dolphin Letters*), Bishop and Lowell's (*Words in Air*), and Lowell's own. Its value is in plotting Hardwick's life and talent, in bringing – in her words – 'a different lighting to the stage'. This is a beginning.

'If humour is allowed into a poem'

Rory Waterman, *Wendy Cope* (Liverpool University Press) £30
Reviewed by N.S. Thompson

Although having paid her dues with magazine appearances, several pamphlets and appearing in Faber's *Poetry Introduction 5*, Wendy Cope's first collection *Making Cocoa for Kingsley Amis* (Faber, 1986) was greeted as if it had sprung from nowhere and several reviewers wished it back there. The reason? Perhaps there were several: she was writing funny (comic) poems, she was using rhyme and metre and she was lampooning or parodying hallowed voices. But she had wit at the end of her pitchfork and the targets were grand enough – or dead enough – not to be affected, or else were tickled by the backhanded compliment in the case of Craig Raine, her editor at Faber; Ted Hughes, the poet laureate; the ever gregarious Peter Porter and the less gregarious Geoffrey Hill. And as these poems would suggest, she fought back at the humourless responses of reviewers in later volumes, especially in the witty 'A Poem on the Theme of Humour' about a poetry contest that excluded it:

> ... if humour is allowed into a poem,
> People may laugh and enjoy it,
> Which gives the poet an unfair advantage.

When one sits through such poetry events as described in 'A Reading', one can see her point. One only has to witness a roomful of listeners doubled up with laughter at one of her readings, to see the advantage is clear. But the flip side of this was depression and anxiety, some of which stemmed from failed relationships. This gave rise to the famous diatribes 'Bloody Men' and 'Rondeau Redoublé', which satisfied some feminists, but not all. However, her difficulties went back to her childhood, a domineering mother and an all too passive father. She underwent therapy in her twenties and has spoken well of it and its efficacy for her. Indeed, her first book was dedicated to her psychoanalyst, a Dr Couch, a classical Freudian, and a case of nominative determinism if ever there was one. The same could be said for Cope herself who has never exploited the name, while having had a

great deal to cope with, as both her earlier poems about men attest, but also the later ones about her family. And is it only me who sees the word 'struggle' in her poetic alter ego 'Strugnell'? It cannot have been easy having a domineering evangelical mother and a father too old to mitigate her excesses (he was fifty-nine when she was born in 1945). Worse was the fact that they demanded she do well at school, but without encouragement for anything beyond that in terms of a career. She gained a place at Oxford, but had a miserable time there, feeling inadequate. Not being a natural rebel, rather having a leaning towards authority, as she has admitted, it took her many years to find herself as a person and as a poet. She was forty before her first collection was published.

Given the overnight popularity with which the work was greeted (albeit not in all quarters), it is also remarkable that Rory Waterman's is the first critical study of her work. As well as submitting individual poems to the fine scrutiny of his jeweller's loupe, he is also able deftly to bring in and, if necessary, rebut earlier assessments of her work in the reviews it received. The format is a simple one of a chapter each on her five major collections, a chapter on her children's verse, ending on a final survey of her uncollected (and some unpublished) work, complete with biographical outline, notes and a select bibliography. Along the way, Waterman takes care to discuss her less characteristic work, as in the narrative 'The Teacher's Tale' (*If I Don't Know*, 2001), a move away from the personal but, as Waterman points out: 'much of Cope's experience is projected into the poem' (p.53). There is a sensitive reading of her book-length narrative poem for children *The River Girl* (1991).

What emerges from the struggles of the earlier work is a highly personal poet. The gibes at men and parodies of their work are gradually left behind as she moves to a closer investigation of herself and her background. On the way, she is brave and confident enough to say how content she is in having finally found love in a suitable man (the poet Lachlan Mackinnon). Contentment is not a popular subject for poetry, but she is able to put on a bravura performance defending her stance in 'Being Boring' (*If I Don't Know*, 2001):

> There was drama enough in my turbulent past:
> Tears and passion – I've used up a tankful.
> No news is good news, and long may it last.
> If nothing much happens, I'm thankful.

As Waterman makes clear, the gratitude is also on the part of her readers.

Ode to the Meanings and Joy of 'Sikfan'

Sean Wai Keung's *sikfan glaschu* (Verve) £9.99
Reviewed by Wendelin Wai C. Law

There is simply no other Cantonese phrase more home-ly and profound than 'sikfan'. When translated literally, it means 'to have rice'. However, it is also used broadly to denote the act of having a meal. It has a third mean-ing, which is explained succinctly by Wai Keung in the title poem, while he conjures a palpable ambience asso-ciated with the phrase:

> then sat by the window thinking about being a kid
>   again [...]
> hearing that familiar evening shout of *sikfan*
>   meaning
> *your food is ready* [...]
>   dont you miss that
> the eagerness/ the hunger/ the sense of mystery
> the not knowing exactly what would be waiting on
>   the table
> but knowing exactly that whatever it was
> it would be delicious

This warm and almost magical scene of 'sikfan' doesn't exist only in the Cantonese-speaking sphere. The collec-tive childhood memory of food and commensality – the act of eating together, are universal and touch all read-ers. As Wai Keung continues to record his gastropoetic ventures, which are spanning across Glasgow's restau-rants and cafés of diverse cultures and heritage, he showcases how food and eating are domestic, as well as communal and political. The poems are reminiscent of an ancient Chinese saying, '民以食為天', meaning 'food is the God of the people': that the people places food before everything else. As apparent as it seems, eating and living are inseparable. It is personal – 'suddenly a memory is evoked / of pizza eaten on the other side of the world' ('byblos cafe'); as much as it is social and relational. Commensality is fundamental to us, and it is especially prominent during the pandemic, when we are suddenly depleted of it – 'my front door to this street here so devoid of people but still littered / with polysty-rene containers almost as if that was all that was left of us' ('wing rush').

Politically, the increasingly globalised century over-shadowed by the lingering aftermath of colonialism, is shown in Glasgow's multi-cultural history as a migrant city. It is evident from the book title itself – *sikfan glaschu* – a hybrid of Cantonese and Gaelic. The opening poem 'chinatown' is a vehement protest for the rightful status

of immigrants in the city – 'this place was built by migrants / therefore it is ours [...] this place was built by migrants / and we have been eating here ever since'. And Wai Keung examines further the product of the diversi-ty and hybridity, which is the questionable authenticity of 'ethnic cuisines'. He urges us to look beyond a fixed definition – 'im always telling people / that chinese food doesnt really exist as a thing / in the same way that brit-ish food doesnt really exist' ('tinto tapas'), and instead, appreciate the inherent joy that 'sikfan' brings us.

sik fan glaschu is a gastropoetic rumination of the meanings surrounding food. Despite its questioning on the definition of identity and authenticity, 'i mean whos to say where exactly it is / that these things really do come from' ('greggs'); despite the undertone of uncer-tainties and the rise of hate crimes during the Covid-19 pandemic – 'if you beat us down in the street / shout profanities at us when we sneeze / blame pandemics on us and our eyes' ('loon fung'); this poetry collection is, all in all, a celebration of care, inclusivity and hopeful-ness – 'that this city really does have amazing italian food / and that sometimes that's enough' ('di maggios').

It is not a lament, but an ode in three parts that are sorrowful and indignant at times, filled with motifs of restless agony and the call for justice in powerful epist-rophes ('pizza hut strathbungo', 'stay inside', 'where is the tree my 公公 drew' and 'time to go'). Just when it seems stifling and disconsolate, Wai Keung never fails to keep striking with words – 'we will not allow you to extinct our bodies // we will not allow you to say that we dont exist' ('loon fung'). His poems are about how 'sik-fan' conjugates and unavoidably embodies so much more than just 'your food is ready'. Like a mesmerised child, never forgetting 'the sense of mystery', he writes with the 'hunger' and 'eagerness' that transform the sadness and fury into uplifting movements, composing this ardent and genial ode to the joy of 'sikfan'.

Life Sentences

Two Twin Pipes Sprout Water, Lila Matsumoto
Path Through Wood, Sam Buchan-Watts
(both Prototype) both £12
Reviewed by Hal Coase

What was irony? Everything new and exciting in these two collections sent me back to Cleanth Brooks's 1949 essay 'Irony as a principle of structure'. The essay gets a few things spot on. Brooks suggests that all statements not limited to 'pure denotations' carry 'an ironic potential': when using language, we either overtly deploy irony or depend upon the tacit understanding that we are not being ironic (irony becomes here a kind of default, the wagging tail of happy language use – this would also explain why explaining irony so often feels like an irrecuperable collapse in communication). Context usually mediates this process for us. But since poems generate their own context, they must, according to Brooks, be capable of controlling this risk: 'invulnerability to irony is the stability of a context in which the internal pressures balance and mutually support each other'. A 'strong' poem can be ironic, it can contain a self-awareness of its own airs and graces, in fact it will need to have as much irony in it as is required to get away with sincerity (this being 'a principle of structure'), but it should never be *vulnerable* to irony outside of its own control, which would threaten to upend the whole exercise. The essay opens by promising irony as raw and riotous potential. It ends with irony tamed at its feet. How come? Did irony scare poets (or critics), once upon a time? Will it come back to haunt us?

Lila Matsumoto writes poems that are vulnerable to irony in ways that I'm sure would have haunted Cleanth Brooks. I'd go as far as to say that she is giving us *structure as a principle of irony* – that is, her collection finds ways to open up interpretative distances and put the text in a frame that will skew any reading too straight. If a certain type of irony – call it jadedness, archness, smugness or snideness – has long been tamed by contemporary poetry, Matsumoto's formal choices signal a committed (you could say sincere) attempt to let irony run wild. Here, for example, are the opening lines of 'In order to make words pleasurable':

In order to make words pleasurable, the fêted author said,
'approach them as spearheads of delicate flint.
Knap them with
antler batons and soft stone hammers.'

The poem closes the collection's first (and best) sequence – 'Pictorial programme' – in which nine scenes are presented across ten- to thirteen-line poems with titles taken from the first line of each. The repetition of the titular lines ('All day the peacocks screamed', 'The dog wanted to go one way') prods us towards the surrealish, whilst the lay of the page put me in mind of gallery labels stripped of all context. Line breaks often serve as ambushes or underscore passing peculiarities (in the lines above, 'knap' takes some thinking once we get 'antler batons'). Then there is the language itself, which often applies a tone I'd call 'collusive' in its sudden attempts to tease out our approval with a common-sensical chattiness ('We all know the sound of wine being poured is sleazy') applied to matters absurdly beyond common-sense or normal chat. The rest of the book makes good on this promise of structural dissonances – ironic sways in tone that want the dreamlike and the banal cheek by jowl. The poems isolate their solitary objects, with minute attention to textures, shades, and

dimensions, only to then pull our attention to the voice we are listening in to.

Sam Buchan-Watts's *Path Through Wood* is likewise concerned with the ironies and surprises of 'listening in' (three poems in the collection share this title). The strongest poem in the book, 'Sounds Inside', is given as '*a private moment splintered with observation*' and considers differing degrees of attention across one excellent fifty-two-line sentence which begins:

I am overhearing a documentary on Radio 4 about music cultures in UK prisons, listening to the
friend I am currently living with, a medical professional at the local prison, listen

as he tries to manage the weekend kitchen, clearing up after his boisterous child, the clamour
of clutter re-joining the kitchen's ambience,

This vertiginous swirl of the concrete and commentary is replicated elsewhere but reaches a high-point here, where allusion and citation compete with 'a rawer / curiosity'. At its best, it's a style capable of demonstrating that attention is a resource like any other (and so: finite, controlled, precious). The poems read like proofs of this idea or, at times, as calls for more careful forms of attention (not only in poetics): 'the onus is nonetheless on you, / … since once an image is seen and lodged / in the mind it can't easily be unseen'. They often begin from paraphrase and push out towards abstraction, or vice versa, as though following Matsumoto's search for 'information recognisable as change'. If paraphrasing a poem is still some kind of taboo (that's Brooks, again), then Buchan-Watts suggests that the act of paraphrasing might itself have some magic to it: 'levels of sound and significance' are enlivened when we ask others to listen in to our listening.

Both poets, then, take the right sort of risks and know that irony should be left to its own devices. The least successful elements of Matsumoto's work are perhaps those where lines or images only seem to bounce off a single incongruity. The sequence 'EyeBread', for example, is a fun game of images, titles, and captions, but without a narrator's lilt breaking in every now and then to muddle things up and thicken out the text with connotations, it can't get much beyond absurdism. In the case of Buchan-Watts, weaker poems ('the art of trying', 'pigeon grey') face the opposite problem: in focusing too tightly on the mannered chit-chat of a narrating subject ('I saw my language like a history of brief romances'), they risk closing themselves off to a richer (and, once more with feeling, *more ironic*) interplay of perspectives. The collections more than make up for these occasional shortcomings, and they offer critical insights into listening and looking, attention and care, with an ironic touch and lyrical flare.

North and South

Jordi Doce, *We Were Not There* translated from the
Spanish by Lawrence Schimel (Shearsman) £12.95
Reviewed by Brian Morton

At the end of 'Aquí, ahora, en ningún sitio' ('Here, Now,
Nowhere'), there is a brief, almost subliminal, possibly
imaginary reference to John the Baptist: '*las mujeres se
cubrían los hombros / y pedían a sus acompañantes / la
cabeza del tiempo*', given by Lawrence Schimel as 'the
women covered their shoulder / and asked their com-
panions / for the head of time'. If the prophet is being
referenced here it squares with an air of suspended wait-
ing, often in desert places, in Jordi Doce's verse. Fore-
running and aftercoming are the essence of many of
these poems. They deal with puzzled, enigmatic journeys
to the north, to cities that the speaker clearly does not
know and to which he has no stated connection, though
there is a woman waiting in 'that weightless town' ('*la
ciudad ingrávida*') at the start of the same poem. Even
she, though, seems to offer nothing explicit.

The pleasure of Doce's poetry, firmly established for
English-speaking readers in *Nothing Is Lost: Selected
Poems,* also translated by Schimel, lies in the way every-
thing is bathed in an 'incomplete light' ('*Una luz incom-
pleta*'), as another poem 'Here' ('Aquí') has it. We are
prepared for stories but they are not delivered. Our lives
seem to be filled with waiting. Writing in *PN Review*

about the selected poems, Ian Seed spoke eloquently
about Doce's 'agnostic faith', which he relates to Paul
Tillich's *Ultimate Concern.* While both phrases sum up
the present collection very neatly, too, there's also a
strong connection to Tillich's later attempts in the post-
humously published *My Search For Absolutes* to redefine
existentialism as merely part of a much larger vision of
creation which doesn't require mankind at all, or cer-
tainly not as a first observer or actor. Doce's poetry
seems to inhabit this same quiet anticipatory realm.

Just as his poetic persona makes journeys to northern
cities, so Doce himself often looks north. He dedicates
a poem to Charles Tomlinson and writes another in the
manner of Penelope Shuttle, a virtuosic set of 'Life
Footnotes' ('Notas a pie de vida') to passages which are,
of course, not divulged to us, which leaves us wonder-
ing who or what is being referenced: '11. He lived hap-
pily until the age of 111 years.', '13. Jazz double bass
player and a mainstay of sessions during the 1990s' (can
he mean Dan Anderson?), '17. Said of the snowbanks
that form on both sides of the path.', '24. All kinds of
rice.' What kind of text would require glosses like
these?

'Life Footnotes' may be an *esprit* but it catches the
strange, occluded vision of Doce's verse very well. There
are prose poems that lure the reader into some expecta-
tion of the discursive, only to confound it, and the vol-
ume ends with a sequence of monostichs (Ashbery is
another of the 'northern' poets referenced), except these
one gain a line as the sequence moves along, playing
with the absence of caesura or significant pause. Num-
ber two brings back the enigmatically 'prophetic' mood
of 'Here, Now, Nowhere': '*Está de pie junto a la puerta. /
Dice: <<Vengo a traerte noticias de tu vida>>.*' ('He stands
beside the door. / Says: "I come to bring you news of your
life".') What is standing 'beside' a door? Is he on this
side, or that? Has he come in, or are we outside? These
are the questions that Doce presses gently on us. Few
modern poets are better able to make us rethink our
everyday purposes and perceptions.

Editors
Michael Schmidt
John McAuliffe

Editorial Manager
Andrew Latimer

Contributing Editors
Vahni Capildeo
Sasha Dugdale
Will Harris

Design
by Andrew Latimer

Editorial address
The Editors at the address on the
right. Manuscripts cannot be
returned unless accompanied by a
stamped addressed envelope or
international reply coupon.

Trade distributors
NBN International

Represented by
Compass IPS Ltd

Copyright
© 2022 Poetry Nation Review
All rights reserved
ISBN 978-1-80017-283-8
ISBN 0144-7076

Subscriptions—6 issues
INDIVIDUAL–print and digital:
£45; abroad £65
INSTITUTIONS–print only:
£76; abroad £90
INSTITUTIONS–digital only:
from Exact Editions (https://shop.
exacteditions.com/gb/pn-review)
to: PN Review, Alliance House,
30 Cross Street, Manchester,
M2 7AQ, UK.

Supported by